Handy Substitutions

Needed Ingredient	Substitution
Baking products:	
Baking powder, 1 teaspoon	½ teaspoon cream of tartar plus ¼ teaspoon baking soda
Chocolate	
semisweet morsels, 6 ounces	6 tablespoons cocoa, 6 tablespoons sugar, plus ¼ cup shortening
sweet baking, 1 (4-ounce) bar	¼ cup cocoa, ⅓ cup sugar, plus 3 tablespoons shortening
unsweetened, 1 ounce or square	3 tablespoons cocoa plus 1 tablespoon butter or margarine
Cornstarch, 1 tablespoon	2 tablespoons all-purpose flour
Corn syrup, light, 1 cup	1 cup sugar plus ¼ cup water
Flour	
all-purpose, 1 cup	1 cup plus 2 tablespoons sifted cake flour
cake, 1 cup sifted	1 cup sifted all-purpose flour, minus 2 tablespoons
self-rising, 1 cup	1 cup all-purpose flour, 1 teaspoon baking powder, plus ½ teaspoon salt
Honey, 1 cup	1¼ cups sugar plus ¼ cup water
Marshmallow cream, 1 (7-ounce) jar	1 (16-ounce) package marshmallows, melted, plus 3½ tablespoons light corn syrup
Powdered sugar, 1 cup	1 cup sugar plus 1 tablespoon cornstarch (all processed in food processor)
Tapioca, granular, 1 tablespoon	1 tablespoon all-purpose flour
Dairy Products:	
Eggs, 2 large	3 small eggs
Milk, 1 cup	½ cup evaporated milk plus ½ cup water
Sour cream, 1 cup	1 cup yogurt plus 3 tablespoons melted butter or 1 cup yogurt plus 1 tablespoon cornstarch
Whipping cream, 1 cup	¾ cup milk plus ⅓ cup melted butter (for baking only; will not whip)
Yogurt, 1 cup	1 cup buttermilk
Seasonings and Spices:	
Allspice, 1 teaspoon ground	½ teaspoon ground cinnamon plus ½ teaspoon ground cloves
Apple pie spice, 1 teaspoon	½ teaspoon ground cinnamon, ¼ teaspoon ground nutmeg, plus ⅛ teaspoon ground cardamom
Brandy, 1 tablespoon	¼ teaspoon brandy extract plus 1 tablespoon water
Ginger, candied, 1 tablespoon	⅛ teaspoon ground ginger
Orange peel, 1 tablespoon	1½ teaspoons orange extract or 1 tablespoon grated orange rind
Pumpkin pie spice, 1 teaspoon	½ teaspoon ground cinnamon, ¼ teaspoon ground ginger, ⅛ teaspoon ground allspice, plus ⅛ teaspoon ground nutmeg
Vanilla bean, 1 (1 inch)	1 teaspoon vanilla extract

Christmas
with Southern Living
Cookbook
Volume 2

Christmas
with Southern Living
Cookbook
Volume 2

*M*ake your holidays magical
with over 200 dazzling recipes, from savory
snacks to scrumptious desserts.

Oxmoor
House®

©1998 by Oxmoor House, Inc.
Book Division of Southern Progress Corporation
P.O. Box 2463, Birmingham, Alabama 35201

Library of Congress Catalog Card Number: 96-72550
ISBN: 0-8487-1696-5
ISSN: 1099-4386

Manufactured in the United States of America
First Printing 1998

Editor-in-Chief: Nancy Fitzpatrick Wyatt
Senior Foods Editor: Susan Payne Stabler
Senior Editor, Editorial Services: Olivia Kindig Wells
Art Director: James Boone

Christmas with Southern Living® *Cookbook Volume 2*
Editor: Julie Fisher
Copy Editor: Keri Bradford Anderson
Editorial Assistant: Alison Rich Lewis
Designer: Alison Turner Bachofer
Illustrator: Travis Tatum
Director, Test Kitchens: Kathleen Royal Phillips
Assistant Director, Test Kitchens: Gayle Hays Sadler
Test Kitchens Staff: Susan Hall Bellows, Julie Christopher, Michele Brown Fuller, Natalie E. King,
    Elizabeth Tyler Luckett, Jan Jacks Moon, Iris Crawley O'Brien, Jan A. Smith
Senior Photographers: Jim Bathie, Howard L. Puckett, Charles Walton IV
Photographers: Ralph Anderson, Bruce Roberts
Senior Photo Stylists: Kay E. Clarke, Leslie Byars Simpson
Photo Stylist: Virginia R. Cravens
Director, Production and Distribution: Phillip Lee
Associate Production Managers: Theresa L. Beste, Vanessa Cobbs Richardson
Production Coordinator: Marianne Jordan Wilson
Production Assistant: Valerie L. Heard

We Want Your Favorite Recipes!

Southern Living cooks are simply the best cooks, and we want your secrets! Please send your favorite original recipes and a sentence about why you like each one. We can't guarantee we'll print them in a cookbook, but if we do, we'll send you $10 and a free copy of the cookbook. Send each recipe on a separate page, with your name, address, and daytime phone number to:

Cookbook Recipes
Oxmoor House
2100 Lakeshore Drive
Birmingham, AL 35209

We're Here For You!
We at Oxmoor House are dedicated to serving you with reliable information that expands your imagination and enriches your life. We welcome your comments and suggestions. Please write us at:

Oxmoor House, Inc.
Editor, *Christmas with Southern Living*® *Cookbook Volume 2*
2100 Lakeshore Drive
Birmingham, Alabama 35209

To order additional publications, call 1-205-877-6560.

Cover: Italian Cream Cake (page 52)
Back Cover: Mediterranean Ravioli (page 137)
Page 2: Chicken Nacho Cheesecake and Crab and Muenster Cheesecake (page 125)

Contents

Introduction

Classic Christmas recipes await you on the following pages. Stir your childhood memories with fresh-baked cookies from this cherished collection. Young and old alike will love these luscious cakes wrapped in velvety frostings and chewy cookies oozing with chips—you'll be tempted to lick the bowl or to snitch some cookie dough. And when the crowd comes by after caroling, pull one of our family favorite casseroles from the freezer, and pop it in the oven. Oh, and don't miss our baking secrets tucked in the back of the book. They promise perfect results every time.

Star-Studded Christmas Cookies,
page 35

Cookies, Cookies, Cookies

Baking cookies is old-fashioned fun. Cookies capture a child's attention and can steal Santa's heart—your kids will be eager to leave a plateful on the hearth for their bearded friend. So preheat your oven, and turn the page.

Chocolate-Filled Meringue Cookies

A squirt of creamy chocolate fills each of these crispy meringues.

    2   egg whites
    ¼   teaspoon cream of tartar
    ½   cup sugar
    1   cup finely chopped pecans, toasted
    1   teaspoon vanilla extract
    1   tablespoon powdered sugar
    ½   cup butter
    2   tablespoons cocoa
    3   tablespoons half-and-half
   2¼   cups sifted powdered sugar

Preheat oven to 350°. Beat egg whites and cream of tartar at high speed of an electric mixer until foamy. Gradually add ½ cup sugar, 1 tablespoon at a time, beating until stiff peaks form and sugar dissolves (2 to 4 minutes). Stir in pecans and vanilla.

Drop mixture by teaspoonfuls onto cookie sheets lined with aluminum foil. Dip finger in 1 tablespoon powdered sugar, and make an indentation in center of each cookie.

Place in oven, and immediately turn oven off. Do not open door for at least 8 hours. Remove from oven; carefully peel cookies from foil.

Combine butter, cocoa, and half-and-half in a small saucepan; bring to a boil over medium heat. Remove from heat, and let cool to room temperature. Gradually add 2¼ cups powdered sugar, beating well with electric mixer.

Just before serving, pipe cocoa mixture (using a pastry bag fitted with a star tip) into indentation of each cookie. **Yield:** 4 dozen.

Oatmeal-Nut-Chocolate Chip Cookies

Dipping these classic cookies in melted chocolate makes them a chocolate lover's dream.

   1½   cups regular oats, uncooked
    1   cup butter or margarine, softened
    1   cup sugar
    1   cup firmly packed brown sugar
    2   large eggs
    1   tablespoon vanilla extract
    2   cups all-purpose flour
    1   teaspoon baking soda
    ½   teaspoon baking powder
    ½   teaspoon salt
    1   (12-ounce) package semisweet chocolate morsels
    3   (1.5-ounce) bars milk chocolate, grated
   1½   cups chopped pecans
   12   ounces chocolate-flavored candy coating, melted (optional)

Place oats in container of an electric blender; cover and process until finely ground. Set aside.

Beat butter in a large bowl at medium speed of an electric mixer until creamy; gradually add sugars, beating well. Add eggs and vanilla, mixing well.

Combine ground oats, flour, and next 3 ingredients; gradually add flour mixture to creamed mixture, mixing well. Stir in chocolate morsels, grated chocolate, and pecans.

Drop dough by heaping teaspoonfuls onto greased cookie sheets. Bake at 375° for 10 to 12 minutes or until lightly browned. Let cool slightly; remove to wire racks to cool completely.

Dip half of each cookie in melted candy coating, if desired; place on wax paper to dry. **Yield:** about 9 dozen.

Chocolate-Filled Meringue Cookies

Oatmeal-Nut-Chocolate Chip Cookies

Best-Ever Chocolate Chip Cookies

This cookie lives up to its name—you'll want to try the flavorful variations, too.

¾ cup butter or margarine, softened
¼ cup shortening
¾ cup sugar
¾ cup firmly packed brown sugar
2 large eggs
1 teaspoon vanilla extract
2¼ cups all-purpose flour
1 teaspoon baking soda
¼ teaspoon salt
1 (12-ounce) package semisweet chocolate morsels

Beat butter and shortening at medium speed of an electric mixer until fluffy; gradually add sugars, beating well. Add eggs and vanilla, beating well.

Combine flour, soda, and salt; add to creamed mixture, mixing well. Stir in chocolate morsels.

Drop dough by heaping teaspoonfuls onto ungreased cookie sheets.

Bake at 375° for 9 to 11 minutes. Let cool slightly on cookie sheets; remove to wire racks to cool completely. **Yield:** about 6½ dozen.

Variations: For **Double Chip Cookies,** prepare Best-Ever Chocolate Chip Cookies, using 1 cup peanut butter morsels or butterscotch morsels and 1 cup semisweet chocolate morsels instead of 1 (12-ounce) package semisweet chocolate morsels. **Yield:** about 6½ dozen.

For **Jumbo Chocolate Chip Cookies,** prepare Best-Ever Chocolate Chip Cookies, dropping them onto ungreased cookie sheets by ¼ cupfuls. Lightly press each cookie into a 3-inch circle with fingertips. Bake at 350° for 15 to 17 minutes. **Yield:** 1½ dozen.

Chunky Chip Cookies

You can freeze these cookies in airtight containers up to three months.

1 cup shortening
1 cup butter or margarine, softened
2 cups sugar
2 cups firmly packed brown sugar
4 large eggs
2 teaspoons vanilla extract
4 cups all-purpose flour
2 teaspoons baking powder
2 teaspoons baking soda
2 cups regular oats, uncooked
2 cups cornflakes cereal
2 cups (12 ounces) semisweet chocolate morsels
1 cup chopped pecans
1 cup flaked coconut

Beat shortening and butter in a large bowl at medium speed of an electric mixer until creamy; gradually add sugars, beating well. Add eggs, one at a time, beating after each addition. Add vanilla, mixing well.

Combine flour, baking powder, and soda; gradually add to creamed mixture, mixing well. Gradually stir in oats and remaining ingredients.

Drop dough by tablespoonfuls 2 inches apart onto ungreased cookie sheets.

Bake at 350° for 10 minutes or until lightly browned. Remove to wire racks to cool. **Yield:** 9½ dozen.

Orange Slice Cookies

1½ cups finely chopped candy orange
      slices
 ¼ cup all-purpose flour
 1 cup butter or margarine, softened
 1 cup firmly packed brown sugar
 ¾ cup sugar
 2 large eggs
 2 tablespoons milk
 2 tablespoons vanilla extract
 2 cups all-purpose flour
 1 teaspoon baking soda
 ½ teaspoon salt
 ½ teaspoon ground cinnamon
 ½ teaspoon ground nutmeg
2½ cups quick-cooking oats,
      uncooked
 1 cup flaked coconut

Combine chopped orange slices and
¼ cup flour in a medium bowl; toss to
coat candy. Set aside.

Beat butter at medium speed of an
electric mixer until creamy; gradually
add sugars, beating well. Add eggs, milk,
and vanilla; beat well.

Combine 2 cups flour and next 4
ingredients; gradually add to creamed
mixture, beating well. Stir in reserved
candy mixture, oats, and coconut.

Drop dough by rounded teaspoonfuls
2 inches apart onto greased cookie
sheets.

Bake at 375° for 10 minutes. Let cool
slightly on cookie sheets; remove to wire
racks to cool completely. **Yield:** 9 dozen.

Salted Peanut Cookies

 1 cup shortening
 2 cups firmly packed brown sugar
 2 large eggs
 2 cups all-purpose flour
 1 teaspoon baking powder
 1 teaspoon baking soda
 ½ teaspoon salt
 2 cups quick-cooking oats,
      uncooked
 1 cup crispy rice cereal
 1 cup salted peanuts

Beat shortening at medium speed of
an electric mixer until fluffy; gradually
add sugar, beating well. Add eggs, and
beat well.

Combine flour and next 3 ingredients; add to creamed mixture, mixing
well. Stir in oats, cereal, and peanuts.
(Dough will be stiff.)

Drop dough by rounded teaspoonfuls
onto lightly greased cookie sheets.

Bake at 375° for 10 to 12 minutes.
Remove cookies to wire racks to cool.
Yield: 7 dozen.

Should You Grease the Cookie Sheet?

- *Some cookie recipes have such a high butter content that you don't need to grease the cookie sheet before baking. If you do, the cookies will spread too thin.*
- *Each of our recipes specifies whether to grease or not to grease.*

Create a Cookie Booklet

- *Nashville food writer and historian John Egerton got the Kentucky Sugar Cookie recipe from his Kentucky pal Pat Ballard. John likes it so much, he includes it in a Christmas recipe booklet that he sends to friends in lieu of Christmas cards.*
- *Create your own Christmas booklet to share your favorite recipes.*

Ambrosia Cookies

Savor this cookie's wonderful blend of ambrosia flavors—citrus, nuts, and coconut. The ingredient list is long, but the results are worth it.

1 cup butter or margarine, softened
1 cup sugar
1 cup firmly packed dark brown sugar
2 large eggs
2 cups all-purpose flour
2 teaspoons baking powder
½ teaspoon baking soda
½ teaspoon salt
1½ cups regular oats, uncooked
1 cup chopped dates
1 cup golden raisins
1 cup flaked coconut
1 cup chopped pecans
1 teaspoon grated orange rind
1 teaspoon grated lemon rind
1 teaspoon vanilla extract
½ teaspoon almond extract
½ teaspoon orange extract
4 dozen candied cherries, halved

Beat butter at medium speed of an electric mixer until fluffy; gradually add sugars, beating well. Add eggs, one at a time, beating well after each addition.

Combine flour and next 4 ingredients; stir well. Add flour mixture and remaining ingredients except candied cherries to creamed mixture; stir well.

Drop by rounded teaspoonfuls 2 inches apart onto lightly greased cookie sheets; lightly press a cherry half into each cookie.

Bake at 350° for 14 to 16 minutes; let cookies cool on cookie sheets 10 minutes. Remove to wire racks to cool (cookies become firm as they cool).
Yield: about 8 dozen.

Kentucky Sugar Cookies

1 cup butter, softened
1 cup vegetable oil
1 cup sugar
1 cup sifted powdered sugar
2 large eggs
1 teaspoon vanilla extract
4 cups all-purpose flour
1 teaspoon salt
1 teaspoon baking soda
1 teaspoon cream of tartar
Additional sugar (optional)

Beat butter and oil in a large bowl at medium speed of an electric mixer until blended. Gradually add 1 cup sugar and powdered sugar, beating well. Add eggs and vanilla, beating until blended.

Combine flour and next 3 ingredients; add to butter mixture, mixing well.

Drop dough by rounded teaspoonfuls onto ungreased cookie sheets.

Bake at 350° for 9 to 10 minutes or until lightly browned. Remove to wire racks; sprinkle with additional sugar while warm, if desired. Let cool. **Yield:** 9 dozen.

Note: Freeze cookies in airtight containers up to 1 month, if desired.

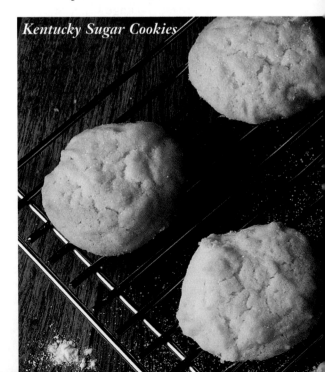
Kentucky Sugar Cookies

Chocolate Macaroon Cookies

1 (4-ounce) package sweet baking chocolate
2 egg whites
½ cup sugar
¼ teaspoon vanilla extract
1 (7-ounce) can flaked coconut

Melt chocolate in a heavy saucepan over low heat, stirring occasionally. Remove from heat, and let cool.

Beat egg whites at high speed of an electric mixer 1 minute. Gradually add sugar, 1 tablespoon at a time, beating until stiff peaks form and sugar dissolves (2 to 4 minutes). Fold in melted chocolate and vanilla. Stir in coconut.

Drop mixture by teaspoonfuls onto cookie sheets lined with aluminum foil.

Bake at 350° for 12 to 15 minutes. Transfer cookies, leaving them on foil, to wire racks; let cool. Carefully remove cookies from foil. **Yield:** 4½ dozen.

Chocolate Crunch Cookies

1 large egg, lightly beaten
1 (18.25-ounce) package German chocolate cake mix
½ cup butter or margarine, melted
1 cup crisp rice cereal

Combine first 3 ingredients, stirring well. Stir in cereal.

Shape mixture into 1-inch balls; place on lightly greased cookie sheets. Dip a fork in flour, and flatten cookies in a crisscross pattern.

Bake at 350° for 10 to 12 minutes. Let cool slightly; remove to wire racks to cool completely. **Yield:** 4 dozen.

Easy Chocolate Chewies

1 (18.25-ounce) package devil's food cake mix
½ cup shortening
1 tablespoon water
2 large eggs
½ cup sifted powdered sugar

Combine first 4 ingredients in a large bowl. Beat at low speed of an electric mixer just until smooth.

Shape dough into 1-inch balls, and roll in powdered sugar. Place 2 inches apart on lightly greased cookie sheets.

Bake at 375° for 10 minutes. Let cookies cool 10 minutes on cookie sheets; remove to wire racks to cool completely. **Yield:** 4 dozen.

Peanut Butter Bars

1 (18.25-ounce) package yellow cake mix
1 cup chunky peanut butter
½ cup butter, melted
2 large eggs
1 cup (6 ounces) semisweet chocolate morsels
1 (14-ounce) can sweetened condensed milk

Combine first 4 ingredients in a large bowl. Beat at medium speed of an electric mixer 1 to 2 minutes.

Press half of mixture into bottom of an ungreased 13- x 9- x 2-inch pan.

Bake at 350° for 10 minutes. Remove from oven; sprinkle with chocolate morsels, and drizzle with condensed milk. Sprinkle with remaining cake mix mixture.

Bake at 350° for 30 additional minutes. Let cool, and cut into bars. **Yield:** 2 dozen.

Cake Mix Cookies

- *Three cookies on this page begin with a cake mix—the ultimate easy baking option. Be creative, and substitute your favorite flavor of cake mix, if desired.*

Graham Cracker–Caramel Bites

This candy-like cookie is easy to make. Just fit the graham crackers snugly in the pan, add the toppings, and bake.

12 double graham crackers
2 cups miniature marshmallows
¾ cup butter or margarine
¾ cup firmly packed brown sugar
1 teaspoon ground cinnamon
1 teaspoon vanilla extract
1 cup sliced almonds
1 cup flaked coconut

Arrange crackers in a greased 15- x 10- x 1-inch jellyroll pan. Sprinkle with marshmallows.

Combine butter, brown sugar, and cinnamon in a heavy saucepan. Bring to a boil over medium heat. Boil, stirring constantly, 1 minute. Remove from heat; stir in vanilla. Spoon mixture over marshmallows. Sprinkle with almonds and coconut.

Bake at 350° for 12 to 14 minutes. Let cool in pan 10 minutes. Cut into 24 squares; cut each square in half to form 2 triangles. Let cool on wire racks. **Yield:** 4 dozen.

Butterscotch Brownies

⅔ cup butter or margarine, softened
1½ cups firmly packed brown sugar
2 large eggs
2 teaspoons vanilla extract
2 cups all-purpose flour
1 teaspoon baking powder
¼ teaspoon baking soda
1 teaspoon salt
1 cup (6 ounces) butterscotch morsels
½ cup chopped pecans

Beat butter at medium speed of an electric mixer until creamy. Add sugar; beat well. Add eggs and vanilla; beat well.

Combine flour and next 3 ingredients; add to creamed mixture, stirring well. Pour batter into a greased 13- x 9- x 2-inch pan. Sprinkle with butterscotch morsels and pecans.

Bake at 350° for 30 minutes. Let cool; cut into bars. **Yield:** 2½ dozen.

Candy Bar Brownies

Substitute your favorite candy bar in this brownie recipe to satisfy your sweet tooth.

4 large eggs, lightly beaten
2 cups sugar
¾ cup butter or margarine, melted
2 teaspoons vanilla extract
1½ cups all-purpose flour
½ teaspoon baking powder
¼ teaspoon salt
⅓ cup cocoa
4 (2.07-ounce) chocolate-coated caramel-peanut nougat bars, coarsely chopped
3 (1.55-ounce) milk chocolate bars, finely chopped

Combine first 4 ingredients in a large bowl. Combine flour and next 3 ingredients; stir into sugar mixture. Fold in chopped nougat bars.

Spoon mixture into a greased and floured 13- x 9- x 2-inch pan; sprinkle with chopped milk chocolate bars.

Bake at 350° for 30 to 35 minutes. Let cool, and cut into squares. **Yield:** 2½ dozen.

Note: For nougat bars, we used Snickers candy bars; for milk chocolate bars, we used Hershey's candy bars.

Cream Cheese Swirl Brownies

1 (4-ounce) package sweet baking chocolate
¼ cup plus 1 tablespoon butter or margarine, divided
½ (8-ounce) package cream cheese, softened
¼ cup sifted powdered sugar
3 large eggs, divided
1 tablespoon all-purpose flour
½ teaspoon vanilla extract
½ cup sugar
¼ cup firmly packed brown sugar
½ cup all-purpose flour
½ teaspoon baking powder
¼ teaspoon salt
1 tablespoon brewed coffee

Melt chocolate and 3 tablespoons butter over low heat, stirring constantly. Set aside to cool.

Beat remaining 2 tablespoons butter and cream cheese in a medium bowl. Gradually add powdered sugar, mixing until light and fluffy. Stir in 1 egg, 1 tablespoon flour, and vanilla. Set aside.

Beat remaining 2 eggs at medium speed of an electric mixer until thick and pale. Gradually add ½ cup sugar and brown sugar, beating until thickened. Combine ½ cup flour, baking powder, and salt; add to egg mixture, mixing well. Stir in cooled chocolate mixture and coffee.

Spread half of chocolate batter into a greased 8-inch square pan. Spoon cream cheese mixture over chocolate batter; top with remaining batter. Swirl batter with a knife to create a marbled effect.

Bake at 350° for 35 to 40 minutes. Let cool, and cut into 2-inch squares. **Yield:** 16 brownies.

White Chocolate Brownies

These brownies are so rich, they don't need a frosting.

⅓ cup butter or margarine
8 ounces white chocolate, chopped and divided
2 large eggs
⅔ cup sugar
1 cup all-purpose flour
½ teaspoon baking powder
¼ teaspoon salt
1 tablespoon vanilla extract
¼ cup sliced almonds

Melt butter in a small saucepan over low heat. Add half of white chocolate, and remove from heat. (Do not stir.)

Beat eggs at medium speed of an electric mixer until thick and pale; gradually add sugar, beating well.

Combine flour, baking powder, and salt; add to egg mixture, mixing just until blended. Stir in melted white chocolate mixture and vanilla. Fold in remaining chopped white chocolate.

Spoon mixture into a greased 8-inch square pan. Place almonds around edge of pan, overlapping to form a border.

Bake at 350° for 32 to 35 minutes. Let cool, and cut into bars. **Yield:** 2 dozen.

The Foil Fix

Here's the secret to beautiful brownies, and it's a breeze.

- *Just grease the pan; then line with a long piece of aluminum foil, allowing foil to extend 2 inches beyond both ends of pan. Grease foil.*
- *Add batter; bake and cool according to the recipe.*
- *Once brownies are cool, lift foil with uncut brownies out of pan. Invert and peel off foil; then turn brownies right side up.*
- *Place on a large cutting board; cut into bars or squares using a sharp knife.*

Mississippi Mud Brownies

4 (1-ounce) squares unsweetened chocolate
1 cup butter or margarine
2 cups sugar
1 cup all-purpose flour
⅛ teaspoon salt
4 large eggs, lightly beaten
1 cup chopped pecans
2 (1-ounce) squares unsweetened chocolate
½ cup evaporated milk
½ cup butter or margarine
½ teaspoon vanilla extract
4½ to 5 cups sifted powdered sugar
3 cups miniature marshmallows

Combine 4 squares chocolate and 1 cup butter in a large saucepan; cook over low heat, stirring until chocolate and butter melt. Remove from heat.

Combine 2 cups sugar, flour, and salt; add to melted chocolate mixture. Add eggs and pecans; stir until blended.

Spoon batter into a lightly greased and floured 13- x 9- x 2-inch pan. Bake at 350° for 25 to 30 minutes or until a wooden pick inserted in center comes out clean.

Meanwhile, combine 2 squares chocolate, milk, and ½ cup butter in a heavy saucepan. Cook over low heat, stirring often, until chocolate and butter melt. Remove from heat. Transfer to a medium bowl. Stir in vanilla. Gradually add powdered sugar, beating at low speed of an electric mixer until frosting is smooth.

Sprinkle marshmallows evenly over warm brownies. Quickly pour frosting over marshmallows, spreading evenly. Let cool, and cut into bars. **Yield:** 2 dozen.

Mississippi Mud Brownie

Peppermint Brownies

4 large eggs
2 cups sugar
1 cup all-purpose flour
1 cup cocoa
1 cup butter or margarine, melted
1 teaspoon vanilla extract
½ teaspoon peppermint extract
Mint Cream Frosting
3 (1-ounce) squares unsweetened chocolate
3 tablespoons butter or margarine

Beat eggs with a wire whisk in a large bowl. Add sugar, and stir well. Combine flour and cocoa; gradually stir into egg mixture. Stir in 1 cup melted butter and flavorings.

Pour batter into a greased 15- x 10- x 1-inch jellyroll pan; bake at 350° for 15 to 18 minutes or until a wooden pick inserted in center comes out clean. Let cool in pan on a wire rack.

Frosted Almond Bar

Frosted Almond Bars

Piping the chocolate on these cookies isn't hard, and you don't need special equipment. Our recipe tells you how to drizzle it from a plastic bag.

  1 cup butter or margarine, softened
  1 cup firmly packed brown sugar
  2 cups all-purpose flour
  ½ teaspoon baking powder
  ¼ teaspoon salt
1½ tablespoons instant coffee granules
  1 cup crushed English toffee-flavored candy bars
  2 (2-ounce) packages slivered almonds, toasted
  1 cup sifted powdered sugar
  2 tablespoons milk
  1 tablespoon butter or margarine, softened
  1 teaspoon vanilla extract
  2 (1-ounce) squares semisweet chocolate

Spread Mint Cream Frosting over brownie layer; freeze 15 minutes. Melt chocolate squares and 3 tablespoons butter in a heavy saucepan over low heat, stirring constantly, until melted. Spread over frosting with a pastry brush. Chill until firm; cut into squares. Store in refrigerator. **Yield:** 2 dozen.

Mint Cream Frosting
  ¼ cup butter or margarine, softened
2¾ cups sifted powdered sugar
  2 to 3 tablespoons milk
  ½ teaspoon peppermint extract
  3 or 4 drops of green food coloring

Beat butter at medium speed of an electric mixer; gradually add powdered sugar, beating after each addition. Add milk, and beat until mixture is spreading consistency. Stir in peppermint extract and food coloring. **Yield:** about 2 cups.

Beat butter at medium speed of an electric mixer until creamy; gradually add brown sugar, beating well. Combine flour and next 3 ingredients; add to butter mixture, beating just until blended. Stir in crushed candy bars and almonds. Spread mixture into a greased 15- x 10- x 1-inch jellyroll pan.

Bake at 350° for 18 minutes or until lightly browned. Combine powdered sugar and next 3 ingredients; spread over warm uncut bars. Let cool in pan on a wire rack. Cut into bars.

Place chocolate in a heavy-duty, zip-top plastic bag; seal bag. Submerge bag in hot water until chocolate melts. Snip a tiny hole in one corner of bag, using scissors; drizzle chocolate over bars. **Yield:** 32 bars.

Cranberry Linzer Squares

Freeze these cookies up to three months, or keep them in a tin for a few days, if desired.

- ½ cup butter or margarine, softened
- 1 (8-ounce) can almond paste
- 1 cup sugar
- 2 large eggs
- 3¼ cups all-purpose flour
- ¼ teaspoon salt
- 2 (9-ounce) jars raspberry-cranberry fruit spread

Beat butter and almond paste at medium speed of an electric mixer until mixture is smooth; add sugar and eggs, beating well.

Combine flour and salt; gradually add flour mixture to almond mixture, mixing well. Reserve 1½ cups. Spread remaining almond mixture in a lightly greased 15- x 10- x 1-inch jellyroll pan. Spread mixture evenly with raspberry-cranberry spread. Cover and chill.

Roll reserved 1½ cups almond mixture between 2 sheets of wax paper to ⅛-inch thickness. Place on a baking sheet; freeze 15 minutes. Remove top piece of wax paper, and cut almond mixture into desired shapes with a 1½-inch canapé cutter. Place cutouts over cranberry mixture.

Bake at 350° on the lower oven rack for 40 minutes or until lightly browned. Let cool, and cut into squares. Store squares in an airtight container up to 3 days. **Yield:** 4½ dozen.

Note: For fruit spread, we used Knott's Berry Farm Light Raspberry and Cranberry Fruit Spread.

Cranberry Linzer Squares

Shortbread Toffee Squares

- 1 cup all-purpose flour
- ¼ cup sifted powdered sugar
- ½ cup butter or margarine, melted
- 1 (14-ounce) can sweetened condensed milk
- 2 tablespoons sugar
- ¼ cup butter or margarine
- ½ teaspoon vanilla extract
- ⅔ cup almond brickle chips
- ¼ cup chopped pecans
- 1 (2-ounce) square chocolate-flavored candy coating, chopped

Combine flour and powdered sugar; stir in ½ cup melted butter. Press mixture into a lightly greased 9-inch square pan. Bake at 350° for 20 to 22 minutes or until browned; set aside.

Combine sweetened condensed milk, 2 tablespoons sugar, and ¼ cup butter in a heavy saucepan; cook over medium heat, stirring constantly, until mixture leaves sides of pan (about 10 minutes). Remove from heat; stir in vanilla. Spread on crust; sprinkle almond brickle chips and pecans over filling. Let stand until firm. Cut into squares.

Place candy coating in a heavy-duty zip-top plastic bag; seal. Microwave at MEDIUM (50% power) for 30 seconds or until chocolate melts. Snip a tiny hole in one corner of bag, using scissors; drizzle chocolate over squares.
Yield: 3 dozen.

Fruitcake Cookies

- 1½ cups finely chopped pecans
- ½ pound yellow candied pineapple, finely chopped
- ½ pound red and green candied cherries, finely chopped
- ½ pound golden raisins
- ¼ cup all-purpose flour
- ½ cup butter or margarine, softened
- 1 cup firmly packed brown sugar
- 4 large eggs
- 2½ cups all-purpose flour
- 1 teaspoon baking soda
- ¾ teaspoon ground cardamom

Combine first 5 ingredients in a large bowl, tossing to coat fruit and nuts with flour. Set aside.

Beat butter in a large bowl at medium speed of an electric mixer until creamy; gradually add brown sugar, beating well. Add eggs; beat well.

Combine 2½ cups flour, soda, and cardamom; gradually add to creamed mixture, beating well. Stir in fruit mixture. Cover and chill.

Divide dough into 3 portions. Spoon each portion onto wax paper, shaping into 12-inch logs. Wrap in wax paper, and freeze at least 24 hours.

Slice logs into ¼-inch thick slices, and place on lightly greased cookie sheets.

Bake at 350° for 6 minutes or until lightly browned. Let cool slightly on cookie sheets, and remove to wire racks to cool completely.
Yield: 9½ dozen.

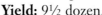

Slice 'n' Bake Savvy

- These slice 'n' bake cookie logs will make many Christmas baking occasions easy for you. They freeze beautifully—just wrap them tightly in wax paper.

- Slice the logs while they're frozen—use a serrated or electric knife for best results.

Peppermint Pats

¾ cup butter or margarine, softened
¼ cup sugar
1 large egg
1 teaspoon vanilla extract
1 teaspoon peppermint extract
2 cups all-purpose flour
½ cup finely crushed hard peppermint candy
Red decorator sugar

Beat butter at high speed of an electric mixer until soft and creamy. Gradually add ¼ cup sugar, beating well. Add egg, beating well. Stir in flavorings. Gradually add flour; mix well. Stir in crushed candy.

Shape dough into 2 (12-inch) logs, and roll in red sugar; wrap logs in wax paper, and freeze until firm.

Slice logs into ½-inch-thick slices, and place on ungreased cookie sheets.

Bake at 350° for 8 to 10 minutes. Remove immediately to wire racks to cool. **Yield:** 4 dozen.

Cinnamon Crisps

½ cup butter or margarine, softened
1 cup firmly packed brown sugar
1 large egg
1 teaspoon vanilla extract
1½ cups all-purpose flour
2 teaspoons baking powder
¼ teaspoon salt
¼ teaspoon ground cinnamon
1 cup ground pecans, toasted
1 egg white, lightly beaten
1 tablespoon sugar
¼ teaspoon ground cinnamon
Pecan halves (optional)

Beat butter at medium speed of an electric mixer until creamy; gradually add brown sugar, beating well. Add egg and vanilla; mix well. Combine flour and next 3 ingredients; stir into butter mixture. Cover and chill 2 hours.

Shape dough into 2 (7½-inch) logs. Roll logs in ground pecans. Wrap in wax paper, and freeze until firm.

Slice logs into ¼-inch-thick slices, and place on lightly greased cookie sheets. Brush each cookie with egg white. Combine 1 tablespoon sugar and ¼ teaspoon cinnamon; sprinkle lightly over cookies, and press a pecan half in center of each, if desired.

Bake at 350° for 8 to 10 minutes or until lightly browned. Remove to wire racks to cool. **Yield:** 5 dozen.

Old-Fashioned Peanut Butter Cookies

1 cup butter or margarine, softened
1 cup creamy peanut butter
1 cup sugar
1 cup firmly packed brown sugar
2 large eggs
1 tablespoon milk
2½ cups all-purpose flour
2 teaspoons baking soda
¼ teaspoon salt
1 teaspoon vanilla extract
  Additional sugar

Beat butter and peanut butter at medium speed of an electric mixer until creamy; gradually add 1 cup sugar and brown sugar, beating until light and fluffy. Add eggs and milk, beating well.

Combine flour, soda, and salt; add to creamed mixture, beating well. Stir in vanilla. Cover and chill 2 to 3 hours.

Shape dough into 1¼-inch balls; place balls 3 inches apart on ungreased cookie sheets. Dip a fork in additional sugar, and flatten cookies in a crisscross pattern.

Bake at 375° for 10 minutes. Remove to wire racks to cool. **Yield:** 6 dozen.

Brown Sugar-Pecan Cookies

1 cup butter or margarine, softened
½ cup sugar
½ cup firmly packed brown sugar
1 large egg
1 teaspoon vanilla extract
2 cups all-purpose flour
½ teaspoon baking soda
¼ teaspoon salt
½ cup finely chopped pecans
  Brown Sugar Frosting
  Pecan halves (optional)

Beat butter at medium speed of an electric mixer until creamy; gradually add sugars, mixing well. Add egg and vanilla; beat well.

Combine flour, soda, and salt; gradually add to creamed mixture, mixing after each addition. Stir in chopped pecans. Cover and chill 30 minutes.

Shape dough into 1-inch balls; place on ungreased cookie sheets.

Bake at 350° for 10 to 12 minutes. Let cool on wire racks, and spread Brown Sugar Frosting over tops. Top each cookie with a pecan half, if desired. **Yield:** 5 dozen.

Brown Sugar Frosting
1 cup firmly packed brown sugar
½ cup half-and-half
1 tablespoon butter or margarine
1½ to 1⅔ cups sifted powdered sugar

Combine brown sugar and half-and-half in a saucepan. Cook over medium heat, stirring constantly, until mixture comes to a boil; boil 4 minutes. Remove from heat. Stir in butter.

Add 1½ cups powdered sugar, and beat at medium speed of an electric mixer until smooth. Gradually add enough remaining powdered sugar to make desired spreading consistency. **Yield:** 1⅓ cups.

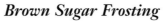

Cherry Crowns

1 cup butter or margarine, softened
1 (3-ounce) package cream cheese, softened
1 cup sugar
1 large egg, separated
1 teaspoon almond extract
2½ cups all-purpose flour
1 cup finely ground blanched almonds
30 red candied cherries, halved

Beat butter and cream cheese at medium speed of an electric mixer until creamy; gradually add sugar, beating well. Add egg yolk and almond extract, mixing well; gradually stir in flour. Cover and chill 1 hour.

Shape dough into 1-inch balls; dip tops of balls in lightly beaten egg white, and then in almonds. Place 2 inches apart on greased cookie sheets. Press a cherry half in center of each ball.

Bake at 350° for 15 minutes. Remove to wire racks to cool. **Yield:** 5 dozen.

Sugar-Coated Chocolate Cookies

½ cup butter or margarine
3 (1-ounce) squares unsweetened chocolate
2 cups sugar
2 cups all-purpose flour
2 teaspoons baking powder
3 large eggs, lightly beaten
2 teaspoons vanilla extract
¾ cup sifted powdered sugar

Melt butter and chocolate in a heavy saucepan over low heat. Combine 2 cups sugar, flour, and baking powder in a large bowl. Add chocolate mixture, eggs, and vanilla, mixing until smooth (mixture will be very thin). Cover and chill at least 2 hours.

Roll dough into 1-inch balls, and roll balls in powdered sugar. Place 2 inches apart on lightly greased cookie sheets.

Bake at 375° for 10 to 12 minutes. Remove to wire racks to cool. **Yield:** 8 dozen.

Cherry Crowns and Sugar-Coated Chocolate Cookies

Mint-Chocolate Snaps

Use mint-flavored chocolate morsels for a double dose of mint.

⅔ cup shortening
¾ cup sugar
1 cup (6 ounces) semisweet chocolate morsels, melted and cooled
¼ cup light corn syrup
1 large egg
1 teaspoon peppermint extract
1 teaspoon vanilla extract
2 cups all-purpose flour
1 teaspoon baking soda
¼ teaspoon salt
¼ cup crushed hard peppermint candy
⅓ cup sugar

Beat shortening at medium speed of an electric mixer; gradually add ¾ cup sugar, beating well. Add chocolate and next 4 ingredients; beat well.

Combine flour, soda, and salt; stir into chocolate mixture. Stir in peppermint candy.

Shape dough into 1-inch balls, and roll in ⅓ cup sugar; place 2 inches apart on ungreased cookie sheets.

Bake at 350° for 12 to 15 minutes. Let cool on cookie sheets 5 minutes; remove to wire racks to cool completely. **Yield:** 5½ dozen.

Spice-Molasses Cookies

This old-fashioned cookie forms a crackled top as it bakes.

¾ cup shortening
1 cup sugar
1 large egg
¼ cup molasses
2 cups all-purpose flour
1 teaspoon baking powder
1 teaspoon baking soda
¼ teaspoon salt
1 teaspoon ground ginger
1 teaspoon ground cinnamon
½ teaspoon ground nutmeg
¼ teaspoon ground cloves
¼ teaspoon ground allspice
Additional sugar

Beat shortening at medium speed of an electric mixer until fluffy; gradually add 1 cup sugar, beating well. Add egg and molasses; mix well.

Combine flour and next 8 ingredients; mix well. Add one-fourth of flour mixture at a time to creamed mixture, beating until smooth after each addition. Cover and chill 1 hour.

Shape dough into 1-inch balls, and roll in additional sugar. Place 2 inches apart on ungreased cookie sheets.

Bake at 375° for 9 to 11 minutes. (Tops will crack.) Remove to wire racks to cool. **Yield:** 4 dozen.

One Spice Fits All

- *Allspice tastes like a blend of cloves, cinnamon, and nutmeg. It's actually a berry.*
- *You can use 1 tablespoon of allspice instead of the five spices listed in Spice-Molasses Cookies.*

Peanut Butter and Chocolate Chunk Cookies

½ cup butter or margarine, softened
¾ cup sugar
⅔ cup firmly packed brown sugar
2 egg whites
1¼ cups chunky peanut butter
1½ teaspoons vanilla extract
1 cup all-purpose flour
½ teaspoon baking soda
¼ teaspoon salt
5 (2.1-ounce) chocolate-covered crispy peanut-buttery candy bars, cut into ½-inch pieces

Beat butter at medium speed of an electric mixer until creamy; gradually add sugars, beating well. Add egg whites, beating well. Stir in peanut butter and vanilla.

Combine flour, soda, and salt; gradually add to creamed mixture, mixing well. Stir in candy.

Shape dough into 1½-inch balls, and place 2 inches apart on lightly greased cookie sheets.

Bake at 350° for 11 minutes or until browned. Let cool 3 minutes on cookie sheets; remove to wire racks to cool completely. **Yield:** 4 dozen.

Note: For chocolate-covered crispy peanut-buttery candy bars, we used Butterfingers.

Shortbread Cookies

¾ cup butter, softened
½ cup sugar
1 egg yolk
1½ cups all-purpose flour
½ teaspoon vanilla extract
Pecan halves (optional)

Beat butter at medium speed of an electric mixer until creamy; gradually add sugar, beating well. Add egg yolk, beating well. Add flour, mixing well. Stir in vanilla.

Shape dough into 1-inch balls, and place on ungreased cookie sheets. Gently press a pecan half in center of each cookie, if desired.

Bake at 300° for 14 to 16 minutes or until lightly browned. Let cool 5 minutes; remove to wire racks to cool completely. **Yield:** 6 dozen.

Shortbread Cookies

Eggnog Logs

Enjoy the mellow flavor of eggnog in this shortbread-textured cookie dipped in Vanilla Frosting.

    1   cup butter or margarine, softened
    ¾   cup sugar
    1   large egg
    2   teaspoons vanilla extract
    1   teaspoon rum flavoring
    3   cups all-purpose flour
    1   teaspoon ground nutmeg
        Vanilla Frosting
    ¾   cup chopped pecans, toasted

Beat butter at medium speed of an electric mixer until creamy; gradually add sugar, beating well. Add egg and flavorings, mixing well.

Combine flour and nutmeg; gradually add to butter mixture, mixing well.

Divide dough into 10 portions. Roll each portion into a 15-inch-long rope; cut each rope into 5 (3-inch) logs. Place 2 inches apart on ungreased cookie sheets.

Bake at 350° for 10 to 12 minutes. Remove to wire racks to cool.

Dip log ends into Vanilla Frosting; roll logs in pecans. **Yield:** 50 cookies.

Vanilla Frosting

    ¼   cup butter or margarine, softened
    2   cups sifted powdered sugar
    2   tablespoons milk
    1   teaspoon vanilla extract

Beat butter at medium speed of an electric mixer until creamy. Add sugar and milk alternately, beating after each addition. Add vanilla; beat until smooth and until mixture is spreading consistency. **Yield:** about 1 cup.

Swedish Heirloom Cookies

    ½   cup shortening
    ½   cup butter or margarine, softened
    1   cup sifted powdered sugar
    ½   teaspoon salt
    2   cups all-purpose flour
    1   tablespoon water
    1   tablespoon vanilla extract
    1¼   cups ground almonds
         Additional powdered sugar

Beat shortening and butter at medium speed of an electric mixer until fluffy. Add 1 cup powdered sugar and salt; mix well. Stir in flour. Add water, vanilla, and almonds, stirring well.

Shape dough into 1-inch balls. Place on ungreased cookie sheets, and flatten.

Bake at 325° for 12 to 15 minutes or until firm and lightly browned. Dredge warm cookies in additional powdered sugar. **Yield:** 4 dozen.

Braided Candy Canes

You can also shape these cookies into wreaths.

¾ cup butter or margarine, softened
1 cup sugar
3 large eggs
1 tablespoon vanilla extract
4 cups all-purpose flour
1 tablespoon baking powder
½ teaspoon baking soda
1 egg white, lightly beaten
Red decorator sugar crystals

Beat butter at medium speed of an electric mixer until creamy; gradually add 1 cup sugar, beating well. Add eggs and vanilla, mixing well.

Combine flour, baking powder, and soda; gradually add flour mixture to butter mixture, beating at low speed just until blended after each addition.

Divide dough into fourths. Divide each portion into 14 pieces; roll each piece into a 9-inch rope. Fold ropes in half, and twist. Shape twists into candy canes; brush with egg white, and sprinkle with decorator sugar crystals.

Place cookies 2 inches apart on ungreased cookie sheets; bake at 350° for 15 minutes or until edges begin to brown. Remove to wire racks to cool.
Yield: 4½ dozen.

Cookie Wreaths

2½ cups all-purpose flour
¼ teaspoon salt
¾ cup sugar
1 tablespoon grated orange rind, divided
1 cup butter or margarine
¼ cup orange juice
1 egg white, lightly beaten
1 teaspoon water
¼ cup sugar
⅓ cup ground almonds
Tube of green decorator frosting
Red cinnamon candies

Combine flour, salt, ¾ cup sugar, and 2 teaspoons orange rind; cut in butter with a pastry blender until mixture is crumbly.

Sprinkle orange juice evenly over surface; stir mixture with a fork until dry ingredients are moistened. Shape dough into a ball; cover and chill.

Divide dough in half. Store 1 portion in refrigerator. Divide remaining portion of dough into 48 balls. Roll 2 balls into 5-inch ropes.

Place ropes on a lightly greased cookie sheet; pinch ends together at one end to seal. Twist ropes together; shape strip into a circle, pinching ends to seal.

Repeat procedure with remaining 46 balls and remaining portion of dough. Combine egg white and water; brush over cookies.

Combine ¼ cup sugar, ground almonds, and remaining 1 teaspoon orange rind; sprinkle mixture on cookies. Bake at 400° for 8 to 10 minutes or until browned. Remove to wire racks to cool.

Pipe holly leaves with green frosting, and top with red cinnamon candies.
Yield: 4 dozen.

Braided Candy Canes

Cookie Wreaths

Costumed Sugar Cookies

1 cup butter, softened
1½ cups sugar
1 large egg
3⅓ cups all-purpose flour
1 teaspoon cream of tartar
½ teaspoon salt
1 egg yolk, lightly beaten
¼ teaspoon water
  Assorted colors of paste food coloring
  Decorator sugar
  Vanilla and chocolate ready-to-spread frosting
  Melted semisweet chocolate (optional)
  Red cinnamon candies (optional)

Beat butter at medium speed of an electric mixer 2 minutes or until creamy. Gradually add 1½ cups sugar to butter, beating mixture well. Add egg, and beat well.

Combine flour, cream of tartar, and salt; add to butter mixture, beating at low speed just until blended.

Roll to ¼-inch thickness between 2 sheets of wax paper. Remove paper; cut with cookie cutters. Place cookies 1 inch apart on ungreased cookie sheets.

Combine egg yolk and water; stir well. Divide mixture among several cups. Tint with desired colors of food coloring. Keep egg yolk paint covered until ready to use. Add a few drops of water if paint thickens too much.

Using a sea sponge or small paintbrush, paint assorted designs on a few cookies with egg yolk paint. Sprinkle a few cookies with decorator sugar. (Some cookies will be baked plain.)

Bake at 350° for 10 to 12 minutes. Let cookies stand 1 minute on cookie sheets. Carefully remove cookies to wire racks to cool completely. Frost plain cookies with vanilla and chocolate frosting, and decorate as desired. **Yield:** 2½ dozen.

Costumed Sugar Cookies

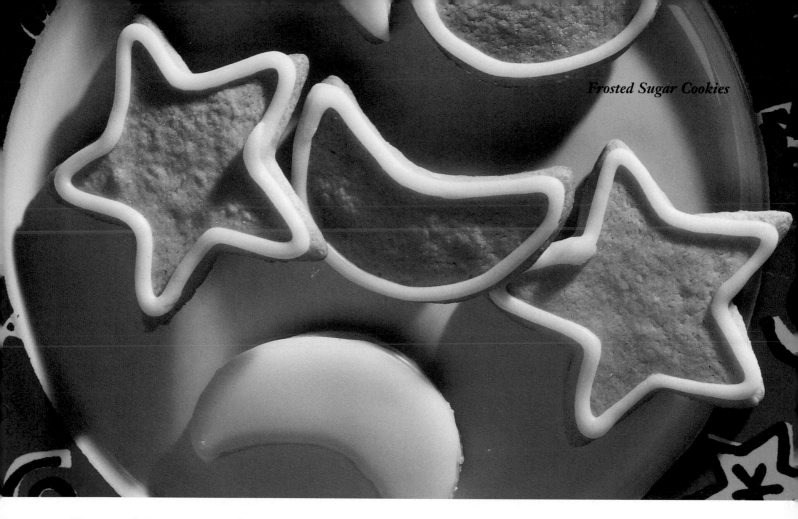

Frosted Sugar Cookies

Each of these snowy white trimmed cookies has only 45 calories—and less than 30% calories from fat.

- ¾ cup plus 2 tablespoons firmly packed brown sugar
- ½ cup margarine, softened
- 1 large egg
- 2 tablespoons skim milk
- 2 teaspoons vanilla extract
- 3 cups all-purpose flour
- 1½ teaspoons baking powder
- ½ teaspoon salt
- 2 teaspoons all-purpose flour, divided
  Vegetable cooking spray
- ½ cup sifted powdered sugar
- 1¼ teaspoons water

Beat brown sugar and margarine at medium speed of an electric mixer until light and fluffy. Add egg, milk, and vanilla; beat well.

Combine 3 cups flour, baking powder, and salt, stirring well; gradually add to creamed mixture, mixing well. Cover and chill at least 2 hours.

Divide dough in half. Work with 1 portion at a time, storing remainder in refrigerator. Sprinkle 1 teaspoon flour evenly on work surface. Turn dough out onto floured surface, and roll dough to ⅛-inch thickness. Cut with a 2-inch cookie cutter, and place 2 inches apart on cookie sheets coated with cooking spray.

Bake at 350° for 6 to 8 minutes or until edges of cookies are lightly browned. Remove to wire racks to cool. Repeat procedure with remaining flour and dough.

Combine powdered sugar and water. Pipe frosting around edges of half the cookies; spread frosting on tops of remaining cookies. **Yield:** 6 dozen.

Gingerbread Boys

- To make small gingerbread cookies, use a 5½-inch cookie cutter; bake at 350° for 8 to 10 minutes. Or use a 3-inch cutter, and bake at 350° for 6 to 8 minutes.

Gingerbread Men

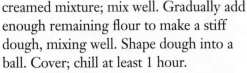

1	cup butter or margarine, softened
1½	cups firmly packed dark brown sugar
2	large eggs
⅔	cup molasses
⅓	cup lemon juice
6½	to 7 cups all-purpose flour, divided
2	tablespoons baking powder
2½	teaspoons ground ginger
2	teaspoons ground cinnamon
½	teaspoon baking soda
½	teaspoon ground cloves
¼	teaspoon ground nutmeg
⅛	teaspoon salt
	Raisins
	Red cinnamon candies
	White Frosting

Beat butter at medium speed of an electric mixer; gradually add brown sugar, beating well. Add eggs, molasses, and lemon juice; beat well.

Combine 2 cups flour and next 7 ingredients; stir well. Add flour mixture to creamed mixture; mix well. Gradually add enough remaining flour to make a stiff dough, mixing well. Shape dough into a ball. Cover; chill at least 1 hour.

Roll half of dough to ¼-inch thickness on a large, greased cookie sheet. Cut gingerbread men with an 8½-inch cookie cutter. Remove excess dough, using the tip of a knife. Add excess dough to remaining half of dough; wrap in wax paper, and chill until needed.

Press raisins and cinnamon candies in each gingerbread man for eyes, nose, mouth, and buttons.

Bake at 350° for 10 to 14 minutes or until golden. Let cool 1 minute on cookie sheet. Remove to wire racks to cool completely. Repeat procedure with remaining dough. Decorate Gingerbread Men with White Frosting. **Yield:** 11 cookies.

White Frosting
1	(16-ounce) package powdered sugar, sifted
½	cup shortening
⅓	cup half-and-half
1	teaspoon vanilla extract

Combine all ingredients in a large bowl; beat at medium speed of an electric mixer until mixture is spreading consistency. Use frosting to outline gingerbread and to make cuffs, collars, belts, and shoes. **Yield:** 2 cups.

Swedish Gingersnaps

1½ cups butter or margarine, softened
1½ cups sugar
1¼ cups molasses
 2 large eggs
 2 teaspoons grated orange rind
 7 cups all-purpose flour
 2 teaspoons baking soda
 1 tablespoon ground ginger
 1 tablespoon ground cinnamon
 2 teaspoons ground cloves
 ½ teaspoon ground cardamom
    Sliced almonds
    Red cinnamon candies

Beat butter at medium speed of an electric mixer until creamy; gradually add sugar, beating well. Add molasses, eggs, and orange rind; mix well.

Combine flour and next 5 ingredients; mix well; gradually add to creamed mixture, mixing until smooth after each addition. Divide dough into 4 equal portions; wrap each portion in plastic wrap, and chill at least 2 hours.

Roll 1 portion of dough (dough will be soft) to ⅛-inch thickness on a well-floured surface; keep remaining dough chilled. Cut with 2- to 3-inch Christmas cookie cutters; place on lightly greased cookie sheets. Decorate with sliced almonds and cinnamon candies.

Bake at 350° for 8 to 10 minutes. Remove to wire racks to cool. Repeat procedure with remaining dough. **Yield:** about 13½ dozen.

Swedish Gingersnaps, above, and Mint-Chocolate Snaps, page 25

Rolled Sugar Cookies

You'll find this to be an easy sugar cookie dough to roll and cut.

- 1 cup butter or margarine, softened
- 1 cup sugar
- 1 large egg
- 1 teaspoon vanilla extract
- 2½ cups all-purpose flour
- 2 teaspoons baking powder
- ¼ teaspoon salt
  Decorator sugar crystals

Beat butter at medium speed of an electric mixer until creamy; gradually add 1 cup sugar, beating well. Add egg and vanilla; beat well.

Combine flour, baking powder, and salt; gradually add to butter mixture, beating just until blended. Shape dough into a ball; cover and chill 1½ hours.

Divide dough into thirds. Work with 1 portion of dough at a time, storing remaining dough in refrigerator. Roll each portion to ¼-inch thickness on a lightly floured surface. Cut with a 3-inch cookie cutter, and place on lightly greased cookie sheets. Sprinkle with sugar crystals.

Bake at 375° for 6 to 8 minutes or until edges are lightly browned. Let cookies cool slightly on cookie sheets; remove to wire racks to cool completely. **Yield:** 3½ dozen.

Star-Studded Christmas Cookies

½ cup butter or margarine, softened
½ cup shortening
1 cup sifted powdered sugar
1 large egg
1 teaspoon vanilla extract
2½ cups all-purpose flour
1 teaspoon salt
  Egg Yolk Paint

Beat butter and shortening at medium speed of an electric mixer; gradually add sugar, beating well. Add egg and vanilla; beat well.

Combine flour and salt; add to creamed mixture, stirring until blended. Divide dough in half; wrap each half in plastic wrap, and chill at least 1 hour.

Roll 1 portion of dough to ⅛-inch thickness on a large, lightly floured cookie sheet; keep remaining dough chilled. Cut with a 3-inch round cookie cutter; remove excess dough. Using a 2- to 2½-inch star-shaped cookie cutter, gently press a star indentation into each cookie. Paint stars and decorative dots on cookies using a small, clean art brush and Egg Yolk Paint.

Bake at 375° for 7 to 9 minutes or until cookies are lightly browned. Remove to wire racks to cool. Repeat procedure with remaining dough. **Yield:** 2½ dozen.

Egg Yolk Paint

1 egg yolk
¼ teaspoon water
  Assorted colors of paste food coloring

Combine egg yolk and water, and mix well. Divide mixture into several cups; tint with paste food coloring. Keep paint covered until ready to use. If paint thickens, stir in a few drops of water. **Yield:** 1½ tablespoons.

Cookie Artistry

• *This egg yolk paint is good to use for any cookie artistry. Just be sure to paint it on the dough before baking. Use only dough that's free of baking powder or soda; otherwise, the design may expand (and crack) as the cookie does.*

Star-Studded Christmas Cookies

Snow Flurries

Snow Flurries

Once you've made your first batch of these cookies, try varying the flavor of jam.

- ½ cup butter or margarine, softened
- ½ cup shortening
- 1 cup sugar
- 2 large eggs
- 1 tablespoon grated lemon rind
- 1 teaspoon vanilla extract
- ½ teaspoon almond extract
- 3½ cups all-purpose flour
- ½ teaspoon baking powder
- ½ teaspoon salt
- ⅓ cup seedless red raspberry jam
- 1 cup sifted powdered sugar

Beat butter and shortening at medium speed of an electric mixer until creamy; gradually add 1 cup sugar, beating well. Add eggs and next 3 ingredients, mixing well.

Combine flour, baking powder, and salt; gradually add to creamed mixture, mixing well. Cover and chill 1 hour.

Divide dough in half; store 1 portion of dough in refrigerator. Roll remaining portion to ⅛-inch thickness on a lightly floured surface. Cut with a 2½-inch star-shaped cookie cutter, and place on ungreased cookie sheets.

Bake at 375° for 7 to 8 minutes or until lightly browned; cool 2 minutes on cookie sheets. Remove cookies to wire racks to cool. Repeat with remaining dough.

Just before serving, spread centers of half of cookies with about ¼ teaspoon raspberry jam. Place a plain cookie on top of each raspberry-covered cookie, alternating points of stars of top and bottom cookies. Sprinkle generously with powdered sugar. **Yield:** 5 dozen.

Mint Christmas Ornament Star Cookies

Peppermint extract is pretty potent. Measure it carefully.

- ¾ cup butter or margarine, softened
- ½ cup sugar
- 1 large egg
- 1 teaspoon vanilla extract
- 1¾ cups all-purpose flour
- 3 tablespoons cornstarch
- ½ teaspoon baking powder
- ⅛ teaspoon salt
- 2 tablespoons sifted powdered sugar
- 2 tablespoons butter or margarine, softened
- 2 tablespoons shortening
- ¾ cup sifted powdered sugar
- 2 teaspoons milk
- ¾ teaspoon peppermint extract
- 3 drops red or green liquid food coloring

Beat ¾ cup butter at medium speed of an electric mixer until creamy; gradually add ½ cup sugar, beating well. Add egg and vanilla, beating well.

Combine flour and next 3 ingredients; gradually add to creamed mixture, mixing well. Cover dough, and chill at least 1 hour.

Roll dough to ⅛-inch thickness on a lightly floured surface. Cut with a 2½-inch crinkled round cookie cutter, and place on ungreased baking sheets. Cut a star shape from centers of half of cookies, using a 1¾-inch star-shaped cutter.

Bake at 350° for 9 minutes or until lightly browned. Remove to wire racks to cool.

Sprinkle cutout cookies with 2 tablespoons powdered sugar.

Beat 2 tablespoons butter and shortening at medium speed; gradually add ¾ cup powdered sugar alternately with milk, beating until smooth. Add peppermint extract and food coloring.

Spread 1 teaspoon peppermint filling onto each solid cookie, and top each with a cutout cookie, powdered sugar side up. **Yield:** 2 dozen.

Whole Wheat Sugar Cookie Christmas Trees

This sugar cookie is made with whole wheat flour. The flavor teams well with raspberry jam.

- ¾ cup butter or margarine, softened
- 1 cup sugar
- 2 large eggs
- ½ teaspoon almond extract
- 1 cup whole wheat flour
- 1½ cups all-purpose flour
- 1 teaspoon baking powder
- 1 teaspoon salt
  Green decorator sugar crystals
- 1 cup seedless red raspberry jam
- 1 (4¼-ounce) tube yellow decorating frosting

Beat butter at medium speed of an electric mixer until creamy; gradually add 1 cup sugar, beating well. Add eggs, one at a time, beating after each addition. Add almond extract, mixing well.

Combine flours, baking powder, and salt; gradually add to creamed mixture, mixing well. Divide dough in half; shape each portion into a ball. Cover and chill at least 1 hour.

Roll 1 portion of dough to ⅛-inch thickness on a lightly floured surface. Cut with a 5-inch Christmas tree-shaped cookie cutter dipped in flour; place cookies on lightly greased cookie sheets. Cut small holes in cookies, using a drinking straw. Sprinkle cookies with sugar crystals.

Bake at 350° for 8 minutes or until lightly browned. Remove to wire racks to cool.

Repeat procedure with remaining dough, but without cutting small holes or sprinkling with green sugar crystals.

Spread one side of each undecorated cookie with 1 tablespoon raspberry jam; top with a decorated cookie. Pipe a star on each cookie with yellow decorating frosting. **Yield:** 16 cookies.

Chocolate-Pecan Torte, page 65

Rave Cakes

What's worth raving about? Just look into the layers of this rich torte smothered in a slick chocolate glaze, or prepare for a bite of a fresh coconut cake that brings grandmother to mind. Let your little ones lick the spatula that overflows with a creamy lump of frosting. And save time with our Fast Frost shortcuts.

Best Butter Bet

• *Real butter makes the difference in these pound cakes; however, you can use margarine in these cakes—it's like choosing between steak and hamburger.*

Cream Cheese Pound Cake

This cake won the highest mark a recipe can receive in our Test Kitchens.

1½ cups butter, softened
1 (8-ounce) package cream cheese, softened
3 cups sugar
6 large eggs
1½ teaspoons vanilla extract
3 cups all-purpose flour
⅛ teaspoon salt

Beat butter and cream cheese at medium speed of an electric mixer 2 minutes or until creamy. Gradually add sugar, beating 5 to 7 minutes. Add eggs, one at a time, beating just until yellow disappears. Stir in vanilla.

Combine flour and salt; gradually add to creamed mixture, beating at low speed just until blended after each addition. Pour batter into a greased and floured 10-inch tube pan.

Fill a 2-cup ovenproof measuring cup with water; place in oven with tube pan.

Bake at 300° for 1 hour and 45 minutes or until a wooden pick inserted in center comes out clean. Let cool in pan on a wire rack 10 to 15 minutes; remove from pan, and let cool completely on wire rack. **Yield:** one 10-inch cake.

Coconut Pound Cake

½ cup shortening
½ cup butter, softened
1 (8-ounce) package cream cheese, softened
3 cups sugar
6 large eggs
3 cups all-purpose flour
¼ teaspoon baking soda
¼ teaspoon salt
1 (6-ounce) package frozen coconut, thawed
1 teaspoon vanilla extract
1 teaspoon coconut flavoring

Beat first 3 ingredients at medium speed of an electric mixer about 2 minutes or until creamy. Gradually add sugar, beating well. Add eggs, one at a time, beating after each addition.

Combine flour, soda, and salt; add to creamed mixture, stirring just until blended. Stir in coconut and flavorings. Pour batter into a greased and floured 10-inch tube pan.

Bake at 325° for 1½ hours or until a wooden pick inserted in center of cake comes out clean. Let cool in pan 10 to 15 minutes; remove from pan, and let cool completely on wire rack. **Yield:** one 10-inch cake.

Chocolate Marbled Pound Cake

½ **cup shortening**
½ **cup butter, softened**
3 **cups sugar**
5 **large eggs**
3 **cups all-purpose flour**
½ **teaspoon baking powder**
¼ **teaspoon salt**
1 **cup milk**
1 **teaspoon vanilla extract**
1 **(1-ounce) square unsweetened chocolate**
1 **tablespoon shortening**
½ **cup chopped pecans**

Beat ½ cup shortening and butter at medium speed of an electric mixer about 2 minutes or until creamy. Gradually add sugar, beating mixture at medium speed 5 to 7 minutes.

Add eggs, one at a time, beating just until yellow disappears.

Combine flour, baking powder, and salt; add to creamed mixture alternately with milk, beginning and ending with flour mixture. Mix at low speed just until blended after each addition. Stir in vanilla. Reserve 2 cups batter.

Combine chocolate and 1 tablespoon shortening in a small, heavy saucepan; cook over low heat, stirring constantly, until chocolate melts. Add chocolate mixture to reserved 2 cups batter, stirring until blended.

Pour one-third of plain batter into a greased and floured 10-inch tube pan; top with half of chocolate batter. Repeat batter layers, ending with plain batter. Swirl batter with a knife to create a marbled effect; sprinkle with pecans.

Bake at 350° for 1 hour and 10 minutes or until a wooden pick inserted in center comes out clean. Let cool in pan on a wire rack 10 to 15 minutes; remove from pan, and let cool completely on wire rack. **Yield:** one 10-inch cake.

Chocolate Marbled Pound Cake

Pound Cake with Easy Caramel Frosting

Spread Easy Caramel Frosting on the cake immediately after it has reached the desired spreading consistency. Otherwise it will become too stiff.

    2   cups butter, softened
    2⅔ cups sugar
    8   large eggs
    3½ cups all-purpose flour
    ½   cup half-and-half
    1   teaspoon vanilla extract
        Easy Caramel Frosting

Beat butter at medium speed of an electric mixer until creamy. Gradually add sugar, beating at medium speed 5 to 7 minutes. Add eggs, one at a time, beating just until yellow disappears.

Add flour to creamed mixture alternately with half-and-half, beginning and ending with flour. Mix at low speed just until blended after each addition. Stir in vanilla. Pour batter into a greased and floured 10-inch tube pan.

Bake at 325° for 1 hour and 15 to 20 minutes. Let cool in pan on a wire rack 10 to 15 minutes; remove from pan, and let cool completely on wire rack.

Spread Easy Caramel Frosting on top and sides of cake. **Yield:** one 10-inch cake.

Easy Caramel Frosting
    ½   cup butter
    1   cup firmly packed brown sugar
    ¼   cup whipping cream
    2½ cups sifted powdered sugar
    1   teaspoon vanilla extract

Melt butter in a heavy saucepan. Add brown sugar; cook over low heat, stirring constantly, 1½ to 2 minutes or until sugar dissolves. (Do not boil.) Remove from heat.

Stir in whipping cream. Add powdered sugar and vanilla.

Beat at high speed of an electric mixer until frosting is spreading consistency. **Yield:** enough for one 10-inch cake.

Pound Cake with Easy Caramel Frosting

Chocolate Fruitcakes

Reduce the butter to ½ cup and the chocolate to 4 (1-ounce) squares to make this rich chocolate fruitcake a little lighter.

  1 cup butter or margarine
  6 (1-ounce) squares semisweet chocolate
1¼ cups sugar
  3 large eggs
  1 cup all-purpose flour
  ¼ teaspoon salt
  1 cup red candied cherries, halved
  1 cup green candied pineapple, cut into ½-inch wedges
  ¾ cup walnut halves
  ¾ cup pecan halves
    Garnish: red candied cherries

Melt butter and chocolate in a heavy saucepan over low heat, stirring often. Remove from heat, and let cool about 15 minutes.

Stir in sugar. Add eggs, one at a time, stirring well after each addition. Add flour and salt, stirring until blended. Stir in cherries and next 3 ingredients. Spoon batter into 4 greased and floured 5- x 3- x 2-inch loafpans.

Bake at 350° for 35 minutes or until a wooden pick inserted in center comes out clean. Let cool in pans on wire racks 10 minutes; remove from pans, and let cool on wire racks.

Seal cakes in heavy-duty plastic wrap; chill 8 hours before cutting. Garnish, if desired. **Yield:** 4 loaves.

Hurry-Up Fruitcake with Lemon Sauce

  1 cup chopped pecans
  1 cup raisins
  1 cup chopped red candied cherries
  ¼ cup all-purpose flour, divided
  1 (16.5-ounce) package date-nut bread mix
  ¾ teaspoon baking powder
  1 teaspoon ground cinnamon
  ¼ teaspoon ground nutmeg
  ¼ teaspoon ground allspice
  3 large eggs, lightly beaten
  ¼ cup water
  ¼ cup orange marmalade
    Lemon Sauce

Line a 9- x 5- x 3-inch loafpan with nonrecycled brown paper; grease paper.

Combine first 3 ingredients; add 2 tablespoons flour, stirring well. Set aside.

Combine remaining 2 tablespoons flour, bread mix, and next 4 ingredients; add eggs, water, and marmalade, stirring well. Stir in fruit mixture. Spoon batter into prepared pan.

Bake at 325° for 1 hour and 15 to 20 minutes. Let cool in pan on a wire rack 10 minutes; remove from pan, and let cool completely on wire rack. Serve with warm Lemon Sauce. **Yield:** 1 loaf.

Lemon Sauce
  ½ cup butter or margarine
  1 cup sugar
  ¼ cup water
  2 teaspoons grated lemon rind
  3 tablespoons fresh lemon juice
  1 large egg, lightly beaten

Melt butter in a saucepan; add remaining ingredients. Cook, stirring with a whisk, 6 minutes or until bubbly. Serve warm. **Yield:** 1⅔ cups.

Old South Fruitcake

Chill this cake, and it will slice neatly and easily.

1½ cups butter, softened
1¼ cups firmly packed brown sugar
⅓ cup molasses
7 large eggs, separated
3 cups all-purpose flour
1½ pounds yellow, green, and red candied pineapple, chopped (about 3¾ cups)
1 pound red and green candied cherries, halved (about 2½ cups)
3 cups pecan halves, lightly toasted
1 cup walnuts, coarsely chopped
¾ cup golden raisins
¾ cup raisins
½ cup all-purpose flour
1 teaspoon ground allspice
¼ cup brandy
1 tablespoon powdered sugar
Additional brandy (optional)

Old South Fruitcake

Draw a 10-inch circle on a piece of nonrecycled brown paper, using a two-piece tube pan as a guide. Cut out circle; set tube pan insert in center, and draw around inside tube. Cut out smaller circle. Grease paper; set aside. Heavily grease and flour 10-inch tube pan; set aside.

Beat butter at medium speed of an electric mixer until creamy; gradually add brown sugar, beating well. Stir in molasses. Beat egg yolks; alternately add beaten yolks and 3 cups flour to creamed mixture. (Batter will be very thick.)

Combine candied pineapple and next 5 ingredients in a large bowl; sprinkle with ½ cup flour and allspice, stirring to coat well. Stir mixture into batter.

Beat egg whites until stiff peaks form; gradually fold into batter. Spoon batter into prepared pan. Cover pan with 10-inch paper circle, greased side down.

Bake at 250° for 4 hours or until cake tests done. Remove from oven. Discard paper cover. Let cool in pan 10 minutes. Loosen cake from sides of tube pan, using a narrow metal spatula; invert pan, and remove cake. Invert cake again onto a wire rack. Combine ¼ cup brandy and powdered sugar; slowly pour evenly over cake. Let cool completely on wire rack.

Wrap cake in brandy-soaked cheesecloth. Store in an airtight container in a cool place 3 weeks. Pour a small amount of brandy over cake each week, if desired. **Yield:** one 10-inch cake.

Variation: To make fruitcake loaves, spoon batter into 3 greased and floured 8½- x 4½- x 3-inch loafpans or 6 greased and floured 6- x 3½- x 2¼-inch miniature loafpans. Bake at 250° for 2½ hours or until cake tests done.

Compromise Cake

This unique recipe doesn't compromise on flavor; it's the perfect truce between a fruitcake and a spice cake.

1½ cups applesauce
1½ teaspoons baking soda
1 cup raisins
1 cup chopped dates
1 cup chopped pecans
½ cup shortening
1⅓ cups sugar
2 large eggs
2 cups sifted cake flour
2 tablespoons cocoa
½ teaspoon salt
½ teaspoon ground cinnamon
½ teaspoon ground cloves
½ teaspoon ground nutmeg
1 teaspoon vanilla extract

Grease bottom of a 10-inch tube pan; line bottom with wax paper. Grease and flour wax paper and sides of pan.

Combine applesauce and soda; set aside. Combine raisins, dates, and pecans; set aside.

Beat shortening at medium speed of an electric mixer until fluffy; gradually add sugar, beating well. Add eggs, one at a time, beating until blended after each addition.

Combine flour and next 5 ingredients; add ½ cup flour mixture to raisin mixture, tossing gently to coat fruit. Gradually add remaining flour mixture to shortening mixture, mixing well. Add applesauce and raisin mixture; stir in vanilla. Spoon batter into prepared pan.

Bake at 350° for 30 minutes. Reduce temperature to 325°, and bake 20 additional minutes. Let cool in pan on a wire rack 10 to 15 minutes; remove from pan, and let cool completely on wire rack. **Yield:** one 10-inch cake.

Chocolate-Toffee Cake

1 teaspoon instant coffee granules
¼ cup boiling water
1 (18.25-ounce) package devil's food cake mix with pudding
3 large eggs
½ cup water
½ cup sour cream
⅓ cup firmly packed brown sugar
2 tablespoons vegetable oil
4 (1.4-ounce) English toffee-flavored candy bars
¼ teaspoon instant coffee granules
1 (1-ounce) square unsweetened chocolate, melted
1 cup sifted powdered sugar
1 tablespoon water
½ teaspoon vanilla extract

Dissolve 1 teaspoon coffee granules in boiling water. Combine coffee, cake mix, and next 5 ingredients, beating at low speed of an electric mixer just until dry ingredients are moistened. Beat at high speed 2 minutes. Coarsely chop candy bars; set aside 2 tablespoons, and stir remaining candy into batter. Spoon batter into a greased and floured 10-inch Bundt pan.

Bake at 350° for 45 minutes or until a wooden pick inserted in center of cake comes out clean. Let cool in pan 10 minutes; remove from pan, and let cool completely on a wire rack.

Dissolve ¼ teaspoon coffee granules in chocolate, stirring until granules dissolve. Add powdered sugar, 1 tablespoon water, and vanilla, stirring until smooth. Add extra water, if needed, for desired glaze consistency. Drizzle over cake, and sprinkle with reserved 2 tablespoons candy. **Yield:** one 10-inch cake.

Almond Cheesecake

40 vanilla wafers
¾ cup slivered almonds, toasted
⅓ cup sugar
⅓ cup butter or margarine, melted
3 (8-ounce) packages cream cheese, softened
1 cup sugar
4 large eggs
⅓ cup whipping cream
¼ cup almond-flavored liqueur
2 teaspoons vanilla extract, divided
2 (8-ounce) cartons sour cream
1 tablespoon sugar
1 tablespoon almond-flavored liqueur
Garnishes: sliced almonds, sliced strawberries, and sliced kiwifruit

Position knife blade in food processor bowl; add first 3 ingredients. Process until crushed. Add butter; process until blended.

Press mixture onto bottom and 1¾ inches up sides of a lightly greased 9-inch springform pan.

Combine cream cheese and 1 cup sugar; beat at high speed of an electric mixer until fluffy. Add eggs, one at a time, beating well after each addition. Add whipping cream, ¼ cup liqueur, and 1 teaspoon vanilla, beating well at medium speed. Pour into prepared crust.

Bake at 350° for 30 minutes. Reduce heat to 225°, and bake 1 hour. Let cool in pan on a wire rack 5 minutes.

Combine remaining 1 teaspoon vanilla, sour cream, 1 tablespoon sugar, and 1 tablespoon liqueur; spread evenly over warm cheesecake. Return to oven, and bake 5 additional minutes.

Let cool in pan on a wire rack 30 minutes. Gently run a knife around edge of cheesecake to loosen; let cool completely in pan on wire rack. Cover and chill 8 hours. Remove sides of pan; garnish, if desired. **Yield:** one 9-inch cheesecake.

When Your Cheesecake Cracks

- *If your cheesecake cracks when it's baked, don't worry. A sour cream topping hides any flaws. In fact, you can spread the sour cream topping from Almond Cheesecake (minus the liqueur) on any cheesecake; then bake it as directed here.*

Almond Cheesecake

Candy Bar Cheesecake

¾ cup graham cracker crumbs
⅔ cup finely chopped walnuts
2 tablespoons sugar
2 tablespoons butter or margarine, melted
4 (3-ounce) packages cream cheese, softened
¾ cup sugar
2 tablespoons cocoa
Dash of salt
2 large eggs
1 (8-ounce) milk chocolate candy bar, melted
½ cup sour cream
½ teaspoon vanilla extract
Sour Cream Topping
Additional chopped walnuts

Combine first 4 ingredients; firmly press mixture into bottom and 2 inches up sides of an 8-inch springform pan.

Beat cream cheese at medium speed of an electric mixer until fluffy. Combine ¾ cup sugar, cocoa, and salt; gradually add to cream cheese, beating well. Add eggs, one at a time, beating after each addition. Stir in chocolate, sour cream, and vanilla, blending well. Pour into crust.

Bake at 325° for 40 minutes. Turn off oven; leave cheesecake in closed oven 30 minutes. Remove from oven, and let cool on a wire rack; chill. Remove sides of pan. Spread cheesecake with Sour Cream Topping; sprinkle with additional walnuts. **Yield:** one 8-inch cheesecake.

Sour Cream Topping
½ cup sour cream
2 tablespoons sugar
½ teaspoon vanilla extract

Combine all ingredients. **Yield:** ½ cup.

Coconut Cream Cheesecake

1⅔ cups graham cracker crumbs
¼ cup sugar
¼ cup plus 2 tablespoons butter or margarine, melted
3 (8-ounce) packages cream cheese, softened
1½ cups sugar
4 large eggs
2 egg yolks
1 cup flaked coconut
1 cup whipping cream
1 teaspoon vanilla extract
½ teaspoon coconut flavoring
Whipped cream (optional)
Toasted coconut (optional)

Combine first 3 ingredients; firmly press mixture into bottom and 2 inches up sides of a 10-inch springform pan.

Beat cream cheese at high speed of an electric mixer until light and fluffy; gradually add 1½ cups sugar, beating well. Add eggs and yolks, one at a time, beating after each addition. Stir in coconut and next 3 ingredients; pour into prepared crust.

Bake at 325° for 1 hour and 10 minutes. (Center will be soft.) Turn oven off; leave cake in oven 30 minutes. Remove from oven, and let cool completely on a wire rack. Cover and chill at least 8 hours.

Remove sides of pan. Top each serving with whipped cream and toasted coconut, if desired. **Yield:** one 10-inch cheesecake.

Italian Ricotta Cheesecake

- ¾ cup all-purpose flour
- 2 tablespoons sugar
- ⅛ teaspoon salt
- ⅓ cup butter or margarine
- 2½ cups ricotta cheese
- ½ cup sugar
- 3 tablespoons all-purpose flour
- 3 large eggs
- 1 teaspoon grated orange rind
- 1 teaspoon vanilla extract
- ¼ teaspoon salt
- 2 tablespoons golden raisins
- 2 tablespoons finely chopped candied citron
- 2 tablespoons chopped almonds
  Garnishes: orange sections, orange rind strips

Combine first 3 ingredients in a small bowl; cut in butter with a pastry blender until mixture is crumbly. Press mixture into bottom of a 9-inch springform pan. Bake at 475° for 5 minutes. Let cool on a wire rack.

Combine ricotta, ½ cup sugar, and 3 tablespoons flour; beat at medium speed of an electric mixer until smooth. Add eggs and next 3 ingredients; beat 4 minutes. Stir in raisins, citron, and almonds. Spoon mixture over crust.

Bake at 350° for 1 hour to 1 hour and 15 minutes or until center is set. Run a knife around edge of cheesecake to loosen; let cool in pan on a wire rack. Cover and chill at least 8 hours.

Remove sides of pan just before serving. Garnish, if desired. **Yield:** one 9-inch cheesecake.

Italian Ricotta Cheesecake

Fresh Coconut Cream Cake

In a pinch for time? Substitute 3 cups canned or frozen coconut for fresh.

 1 cup butter or margarine, softened
 2 cups sugar
 3 large eggs
 3 cups all-purpose flour
 2 teaspoons baking powder
 1 cup milk
 1 teaspoon vanilla extract
 1 teaspoon lemon extract
 ½ teaspoon butter flavoring
 ½ cup water
 1 tablespoon sugar
    White Frosting
 1 (1¼-pound) fresh coconut, grated

Beat butter at medium speed of an electric mixer until creamy. Gradually add 2 cups sugar, beating well. Add eggs, one at a time; beat after each addition.

Combine flour and baking powder; add to creamed mixture alternately with milk, beginning and ending with flour mixture. Mix after each addition. Stir in flavorings. Pour batter into 3 greased and floured 9-inch round cakepans.

Bake at 350° for 25 to 30 minutes or until a wooden pick inserted in center comes out clean. Let cool in pans on wire racks 10 minutes; remove from pans, and cool completely on wire racks.

Combine water and 1 tablespoon sugar in a small saucepan. Bring to a boil; reduce heat, and simmer 3 minutes. Drizzle over cake layers.

Spread about 1 cup White Frosting between layers, sprinkling ½ cup coconut between each layer. Spread top and sides with remaining 3 cups White Frosting, and sprinkle with remaining coconut. Store in refrigerator. **Yield:** one 3-layer cake.

White Frosting
 2 cups whipping cream
 ½ cup sugar
 1 teaspoon vanilla extract
 1 teaspoon lemon extract
 2 drops butter flavoring

Combine all ingredients; beat at medium speed of electric mixer until soft peaks form. **Yield:** 4 cups.

Italian Cream Cake

This moist cake coated with cream cheese is best if made a day ahead and chilled. It's easier to cut, too.

 ½ cup shortening
 ½ cup butter or margarine, softened
 2 cups sugar
 5 large eggs
 2 cups all-purpose flour
 1 teaspoon baking soda
 1 cup buttermilk
 1 teaspoon vanilla extract
 1 (3½-ounce) can flaked coconut
 1 cup chopped pecans
    Cream Cheese Frosting

Beat shortening and butter at medium speed of an electric mixer until fluffy; gradually add sugar, beating well. Add eggs, one at a time, beating after each addition.

Combine flour and soda; add to creamed mixture alternately with buttermilk, beginning and ending with flour mixture. Mix after each addition. Stir in vanilla, coconut, and pecans. Pour batter into 3 greased and floured 9-inch round cakepans.

Bake at 350° for 20 to 25 minutes or until a wooden pick inserted in center comes out clean. Let cool in pans on

Fast Frost

- We give you fabulous frosting recipes for the layer cakes in this chapter, but we also offer shortcuts. Look for "Fast Frost" suggestions throughout that give a canned frosting substitute.

wire racks 10 minutes; remove from pans, and cool completely on wire racks.

Spread Cream Cheese Frosting between layers and on top and sides of cake. Store cake in refrigerator. **Yield:** one 3-layer cake.

Cream Cheese Frosting

- ⅓ cup butter or margarine, softened
- 1 (8-ounce) package cream cheese, softened
- 1 (3-ounce) package cream cheese, softened
- 6½ cups sifted powdered sugar
- 1½ teaspoons vanilla extract

Beat butter and cream cheeses in a large mixing bowl at medium speed of electric mixer until creamy; gradually add sifted powdered sugar, beating until mixture is smooth. Stir in vanilla. **Yield:** enough for one 3-layer cake.

Fast Frost

- *Substitute 2 (16-ounce) cans cream cheese-flavored frosting for Cream Cheese Frosting in Italian Cream Cake.*

Italian Cream Cake

Lane Cake

1 cup butter or margarine,
    softened
2 cups sugar
3 cups sifted cake flour
1 tablespoon plus 1 teaspoon baking
    powder
¾ cup milk
½ teaspoon vanilla extract
¼ teaspoon almond extract
8 egg whites
    Lane Cake Filling
    Seven-Minute Frosting

Beat butter at medium speed of an electric mixer until creamy; gradually add sugar, beating well.

Combine flour and baking powder; add to creamed mixture alternately with milk, beginning and ending with flour mixture. Mix at low speed after each addition. Stir in flavorings.

Beat egg whites at high speed until peaks form; fold into batter. Pour into 3 greased and floured 9-inch round cakepans.

Bake at 325° for 18 minutes or until a wooden pick inserted in center comes out clean. Let cool in pans on wire racks 10 minutes; remove from pans, and let cool completely on wire racks.

Spread Lane Cake Filling between layers and on top of cake. Spread Seven-Minute Frosting on sides of cake. **Yield:** one 3-layer cake.

Lane Cake Filling

½ cup butter or margarine
8 egg yolks
1½ cups sugar
1 cup chopped pecans
1 cup chopped raisins
1 cup flaked coconut
½ cup chopped maraschino cherries
⅓ cup bourbon or sherry

Melt butter in a heavy saucepan over low heat. Add egg yolks and sugar; cook, stirring vigorously, until sugar dissolves and mixture thickens (18 to 20 minutes). Remove from heat; stir in pecans and remaining ingredients. Let cool completely. **Yield:** 3½ cups.

Seven-Minute Frosting

1½ cups sugar
⅓ cup warm water
2 egg whites
1 tablespoon light corn syrup
1 teaspoon vanilla extract

Combine first 4 ingredients in top of a large double boiler; beat at low speed of an electric mixer 30 seconds or until blended.

Place over boiling water; beat constantly at high speed 7 to 9 minutes or until stiff peaks form and temperature reaches 160°. Remove from heat. Add vanilla; beat 2 minutes or until frosting is spreading consistency. **Yield:** 4½ cups.

Prune Spice Cake

The brown sugar in Sea Foam Frosting gives it a pretty pale brown color.

1 cup water
1 cup chopped prunes
½ cup shortening
1½ cups sugar
3 large eggs
2 cups all-purpose flour
1 teaspoon baking soda
½ teaspoon baking powder
½ teaspoon salt
1½ teaspoons ground cinnamon
1 teaspoon ground nutmeg
1 teaspoon ground allspice
1 cup buttermilk
Sea Foam Frosting

Combine water and prunes in a small saucepan; bring to a boil. Reduce heat, and simmer 8 minutes, stirring often; drain and let cool.

Beat shortening at medium speed of an electric mixer until fluffy; gradually add sugar, beating well. Add eggs, one at a time, beating after each addition. Stir in prunes.

Combine flour and next 6 ingredients; add to creamed mixture alternately with buttermilk, beginning and ending with flour mixture. Mix at low speed after each addition just until blended. Pour batter into 2 greased and floured 9-inch round cakepans.

Bake at 350° for 25 to 30 minutes or until a wooden pick inserted in center comes out clean. Let cool in pans on wire racks 10 minutes; remove from pans, and cool completely on wire racks.

Spread Sea Foam Frosting between layers and on top and sides of cake. **Yield:** one 2-layer cake.

Sea Foam Frosting

1½ cups firmly packed brown
   sugar
¼ cup plus 1 tablespoon warm
   water
1½ teaspoons dark corn syrup
⅛ teaspoon salt
2 egg whites
1 teaspoon vanilla extract

Combine first 5 ingredients in top of a large double boiler; beat at low speed of an electric mixer 30 seconds or until blended.

Place over boiling water; beat constantly at high speed 7 minutes or until temperature reaches 160°. Remove from heat.

Add vanilla; beat 1 to 2 minutes or until frosting is spreading consistency. **Yield:** enough for one 2-layer cake.

Black Walnut Spice Cake

Black Walnut Spice Cake

Black walnuts give this traditional cake a distinctive flavor. Substitute English walnuts or pecans for a milder bite.

1½ cups boiling water
1 cup chopped black walnuts
½ cup shortening
½ cup butter or margarine, softened
2 cups firmly packed light brown sugar
3 large eggs
3 cups all-purpose flour
1 tablespoon baking powder
Dash of salt
½ teaspoon ground cinnamon
½ teaspoon ground nutmeg
½ teaspoon ground cloves
1 cup milk
Buttery Cinnamon Frosting
Additional chopped black walnuts

Combine boiling water and 1 cup walnuts; let stand 5 minutes. Drain well; set aside.

Beat shortening and butter at medium speed of an electric mixer in a large mixing bowl until creamy; gradually add brown sugar, beating well. Add eggs, one at a time, beating until blended after each addition.

Combine flour and next 5 ingredients; add to creamed mixture alternately with milk, beginning and ending with flour mixture. Mix at low speed after each addition just until blended.

Fold in prepared walnuts. Pour batter into 3 greased and floured 9-inch round cakepans.

Bake at 350° for 20 to 25 minutes or until a wooden pick inserted in center comes out clean. Let cool in pans on wire racks 10 minutes; remove from pans, and cool completely on wire racks.

Spread Buttery Cinnamon Frosting between layers and on top and sides of cake. Sprinkle top with additional walnuts. **Yield:** one 3-layer cake.

Buttery Cinnamon Frosting
1 cup butter or margarine, softened
7½ cups sifted powdered sugar, divided
1¼ teaspoons ground cinnamon
¼ cup plus 1 tablespoon milk
2½ teaspoons vanilla extract

Beat butter at high speed of an electric mixer until creamy. Combine 2 cups powdered sugar and cinnamon; add to butter, and beat at medium speed until smooth.

Add remaining 5½ cups sugar to creamed mixture alternately with milk, beating well after each addition. Add vanilla; beat until blended. **Yield:** enough for one 3-layer cake.

It's always a good idea to brush loose crumbs from cake layers before frosting a cake.

Fast Frost
• Substitute 2 (16-ounce) cans vanilla or buttercream frosting for Buttery Cinnamon Frosting; stir in 1¼ teaspoons ground cinnamon.

Peppermint Drum Cake

Peppermint Drum Cake

²⁄₃ **cup shortening**
1³⁄₄ **cups sugar**
3 **cups sifted cake flour**
1 **tablespoon baking powder**
¹⁄₂ **teaspoon salt**
1¹⁄₃ **cups milk**
1 **teaspoon vanilla extract**
4 **egg whites**
Peppermint Glaze
Fluffy Frosting
¹⁄₂ **cup crushed peppermint candy, divided**
Peppermint sticks
Round peppermint candy

Beat shortening at medium speed of an electric mixer until fluffy; gradually add sugar, beating well. Combine flour, baking powder, and salt. Add to creamed mixture alternately with milk, beginning and ending with flour mixture. Mix after each addition. Stir in vanilla.

Beat egg whites at high speed of an electric mixer until stiff peaks form; gently fold into batter. Pour batter into 3 greased and floured 9-inch round cakepans.

Bake at 350° for 20 minutes or until a wooden pick inserted in center comes out clean. Let cool in pans on wire racks 10 minutes. Remove from pans, and let cool 10 minutes on wire racks. Prick warm cake layers at 1-inch intervals with a fork. Spoon Peppermint Glaze over layers; let cool completely.

Place 1 cake layer on plate. Spread with 1 cup Fluffy Frosting, and sprinkle with 2 tablespoons crushed peppermint candy. Repeat with second cake layer. Add third cake layer, and frost top and sides of cake with remaining 3 cups Fluffy Frosting. Sprinkle remaining ¹⁄₄ cup crushed peppermint around edge of cake top, making a 2-inch band. Place peppermint sticks in a zigzag pattern around sides of cake. Place round peppermints at points where peppermint sticks meet. **Yield:** one 3-layer cake.

Peppermint Glaze
¹⁄₃ **cup butter or margarine, melted**
1 **cup sugar**
¹⁄₃ **cup milk**
¹⁄₂ **teaspoon peppermint extract**

Combine all ingredients in a small saucepan. Bring to a boil, stirring constantly, and cook, stirring constantly, 1 minute. **Yield:** 1 cup.

Fluffy Frosting
1¹⁄₂ **cups sugar**
¹⁄₂ **teaspoon cream of tartar**
¹⁄₂ **cup water**
3 **egg whites**
1 **teaspoon vanilla extract**

Combine first 3 ingredients in a saucepan. Cook, stirring constantly, over medium heat until sugar dissolves. Cook, without stirring, to soft ball stage (until candy thermometer registers 240°).

Beat egg whites at high speed of an electric mixer until soft peaks form; continue beating, adding sugar syrup mixture in a heavy stream. Add vanilla; beat until stiff peaks form and frosting is spreading consistency. **Yield:** 5 cups.

Black Forest Cake

2 cups sifted cake flour
1¼ teaspoons baking powder
¼ teaspoon baking soda
¾ teaspoon salt
2 cups sugar
¾ cup cocoa
½ cup shortening
½ cup sour cream, divided
½ cup milk
⅓ cup kirsch or other
   cherry-flavored brandy
2 large eggs
2 egg yolks
4 cups whipping cream
⅓ cup sifted powdered sugar
2 tablespoons kirsch or other
   cherry-flavored brandy
2 (21-ounce) cans cherry pie
   filling

Grease 2 (9-inch) round cakepans. Line bottoms of pans with wax paper; grease wax paper. Flour wax paper and sides of pans. Set aside.

Combine first 6 ingredients in a large mixing bowl; stir well. Add shortening and ¼ cup sour cream. Beat at low speed of an electric mixer 30 seconds or until dry ingredients are moistened. Add remaining ¼ cup sour cream, milk, and ⅓ cup kirsch. Beat at medium speed for 1½ minutes. Add eggs and egg yolks, one at a time, beating 20 seconds after each addition. Pour batter into prepared pans.

Bake at 350° for 30 to 35 minutes or until a wooden pick inserted in center comes out clean. Let cool in pans 10 minutes; remove from pans. Peel off wax paper, and let cake layers cool on wire racks. Split cake layers in half horizontally to make 4 layers. Position knife blade in food processor bowl.

Break 1 cake layer into pieces (photo A); place in bowl, and pulse 5 or 6 times or until cake resembles fine crumbs. Set aside.

Beat whipping cream until foamy; gradually add powdered sugar, beating until soft peaks form. Add 2 tablespoons kirsch, beating until stiff peaks form. Reserve 1½ cups whipped cream.

Place 1 cake layer on a cake plate; spread with 1 cup whipped cream, and top with 1 cup pie filling. Repeat procedure once, and top with remaining cake layer. Frost top and sides of cake with whipped cream. Pat cake crumbs around sides of frosted cake (photo B). Pipe or spoon reserved 1½ cups whipped cream around top edges of cake; spoon 1 cup pie filling in center. (Reserve any remaining pie filling for other uses.) Cover and chill cake 8 hours before serving. **Yield:** one 3-layer cake.

Fast Frost

- Use 1½ cups commercial buttercream frosting in lieu of Almond Cream Filling. Just stir in ½ teaspoon almond extract before spreading on cake.

Cocoa Layer Cake

½ cup cocoa
½ cup boiling water
⅔ cup shortening
1¾ cups sugar
2 large eggs
2¼ cups all-purpose flour
1½ teaspoons baking soda
¼ teaspoon salt
1½ cups buttermilk
1 teaspoon vanilla extract
Almond Cream Filling
Chocolate Frosting
Garnishes: toasted sliced almonds, candied violets

Grease 3 (8-inch) round cakepans. Line bottoms of pans with wax paper; grease wax paper. Flour wax paper and sides of pans. Set aside.

Combine cocoa and boiling water in a small bowl; stir until smooth. Beat shortening at medium speed of an electric mixer until creamy; gradually add sugar, beating well. Add eggs, one at a time, beating after each addition.

Combine flour, soda, and salt; add to creamed mixture alternately with buttermilk, beginning and ending with flour mixture. Mix after each addition. Stir in cocoa mixture and vanilla. Pour batter into prepared pans.

Bake at 350° for 25 minutes or until a wooden pick inserted in center comes out clean. Let cool in pans on wire racks 10 minutes; remove from pans, and let cool completely on wire racks.

Spread Almond Cream Filling between layers to within ½ inch of edge. Reserve 1 cup Chocolate Frosting; spread remaining frosting on top and sides of cake. Using a star tip, pipe reserved frosting on top of cake. Garnish, if desired. **Yield:** one 3-layer cake.

Almond Cream Filling

2 tablespoons all-purpose flour
¼ cup plus 1 tablespoon milk
¼ cup shortening
2 tablespoons butter or margarine, softened
½ teaspoon almond extract
⅛ teaspoon salt
2 cups sifted powdered sugar

Combine flour and milk in a small saucepan; cook over low heat, stirring constantly with a wire whisk, until mixture is thick enough to hold its shape and resembles a soft frosting. (Do not boil.) Remove from heat, and let cool completely.

Beat shortening and butter at medium speed of an electric mixer until creamy; add flour mixture, extract, and salt, beating well. Gradually add powdered sugar; beat at high speed 4 to 5 minutes or until fluffy. **Yield:** 1½ cups.

Chocolate Frosting

½ cup butter or margarine, softened
3 (1-ounce) squares unsweetened chocolate, melted
½ cup milk
1 teaspoon vanilla extract
1 (16-ounce) package powdered sugar, sifted

Beat butter at medium speed of an electric mixer until creamy. Add chocolate, milk, and vanilla; beat well. Gradually add sugar; beat at high speed 5 minutes or until frosting is spreading consistency. **Yield:** enough for one 3-layer cake.

Chocolate-Almond Cake

Brownie mix is the secret ingredient in this elegant, speedy cake.

- 1 (23.5-ounce) package brownie mix with chocolate pieces
- ¼ cup water
- 3 large eggs
- 1 cup whipping cream
- ¼ cup sifted powdered sugar
- ½ teaspoon almond extract
  Chocolate Glaze
- ½ cup sliced almonds, toasted

Combine brownie mix, water, and eggs, stirring until blended; pour into 3 greased and floured 8-inch round cakepans.

Bake at 350° for 12 minutes. Let cool in pans on wire racks 10 minutes; remove from pans, and let cool completely on wire racks.

Beat whipping cream at medium speed of an electric mixer until foamy; gradually add powdered sugar, beating until stiff peaks form. Stir in almond extract. Spread filling between layers.

Spread Chocolate Glaze on top and sides. Arrange almonds around sides, covering spaces between layers. Store in refrigerator. **Yield:** one 8-inch cake.

Chocolate Glaze

- ¼ cup cocoa
- 3 tablespoons water
- 2 tablespoons vegetable oil
- 2 tablespoons corn syrup
- 2 cups sifted powdered sugar

Combine first 4 ingredients in a small saucepan. Cook over low heat, stirring constantly, 2 minutes or until smooth. Remove from heat, and stir in powdered sugar. **Yield:** 1 cup.

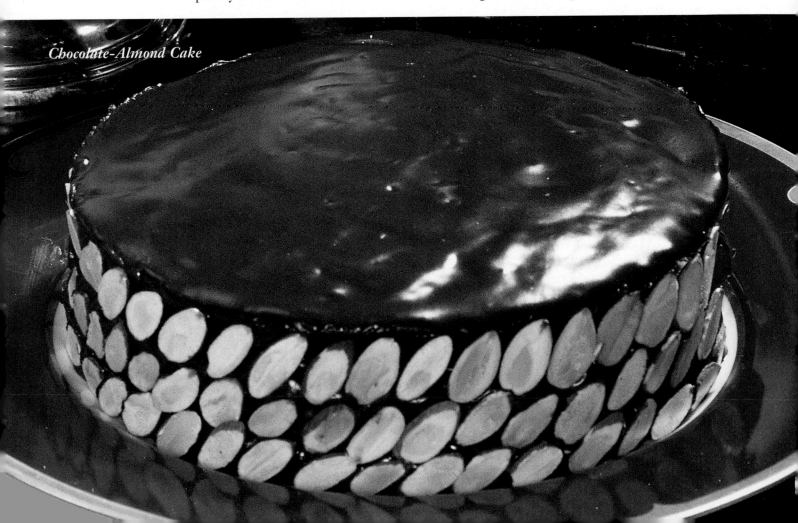

Chocolate-Almond Cake

Chocolate-Pecan Torte

4 large eggs, separated
½ cup sugar
⅔ cup all-purpose flour
½ teaspoon baking soda
¼ teaspoon salt
¾ cup ground pecans
⅓ cup cocoa
¼ cup water
1 teaspoon vanilla extract
¼ cup sugar
   Chocolate Frosting
¾ cup chopped pecans, toasted
   Rich Chocolate Glaze
   Garnish: chocolate leaves

Chocolate-Pecan Torte

Grease bottoms of 2 (9-inch) round cakepans. Line bottoms of pans with wax paper; grease wax paper. Set aside.

Beat egg yolks at high speed of an electric mixer; gradually add ½ cup sugar, beating until mixture is thick and pale. Combine flour and next 4 ingredients; add to yolk mixture alternately with water, beginning and ending with flour mixture. Stir in vanilla.

Beat egg whites at high speed of an electric mixer until foamy; gradually add ¼ cup sugar, beating until stiff peaks form. Fold into batter. Pour batter into prepared pans.

Bake at 375° for 16 to 18 minutes or until a wooden pick inserted in center comes out clean. Let cool in pans on wire racks 10 minutes; remove from pans, and cool completely on wire racks.

Split cake layers in half horizontally to make 4 layers. Place 1 layer on a serving plate; spread 1 cup Chocolate Frosting on top of layer. Repeat procedure with second and third layers and 2 additional cups frosting. Top stack with fourth cake layer. Spread remaining ½ cup frosting on sides of cake; press

chopped pecans into frosting. Spread Rich Chocolate Glaze over top. Garnish, if desired. **Yield:** one 9-inch cake.

Chocolate Frosting
⅔ cup sifted powdered sugar
⅓ cup cocoa
2 cups whipping cream
1½ teaspoons vanilla extract

Combine sugar and cocoa; gradually stir in cream and vanilla. Beat at low speed of an electric mixer until mixture is blended; then beat at high speed until stiff peaks form. **Yield:** 3½ cups.

Rich Chocolate Glaze
2 tablespoons cocoa
2 tablespoons water
1 tablespoon butter or margarine
1 cup sifted powdered sugar
¼ teaspoon vanilla extract

Combine first 3 ingredients in a small saucepan; cook over medium heat, stirring constantly, until mixture thickens. Remove from heat; stir in powdered sugar and vanilla. **Yield:** ⅓ cup.

Bûche de Noël

Bûche de Noël

Vegetable oil
4 large eggs, separated
¼ cup sugar
1 tablespoon vegetable oil
1 teaspoon almond extract
½ cup sugar
⅔ cup sifted cake flour
1 teaspoon baking powder
¼ teaspoon salt
2 tablespoons powdered sugar
Amaretto Filling
Mocha Buttercream Frosting
Garnishes: chocolate leaves,
   cranberries

Grease bottom and sides of a 15- x 10- x 1-inch jellyroll pan with vegetable oil; line with wax paper, and grease and flour wax paper. Set aside.

Beat egg yolks in a large mixing bowl at high speed of an electric mixer until thick and pale. Gradually add ¼ cup sugar, beating constantly. Stir in 1 tablespoon vegetable oil and almond extract.

Beat egg whites at high speed until foamy. Gradually add ½ cup sugar, 1 tablespoon at a time, beating until stiff peaks form. Fold egg white mixture into yolk mixture.

Combine flour, baking powder, and salt; fold into egg mixture, and spread batter evenly into prepared pan.

Bake at 350° for 8 to 10 minutes. Sift powdered sugar in a 15- x 10-inch rectangle on a cloth towel. When cake is done, immediately loosen from sides of pan; turn out onto sugar-coated towel. Peel off wax paper. Starting at narrow end, roll up cake and towel together; cool completely on a wire rack, seam side down.

Unroll cake; spread with Amaretto Filling, and reroll without towel. Place on a serving plate, seam side down.

Cut a 1-inch piece diagonally from one end of cake. Position short piece against top center of longer piece, cut side up, to resemble the knot of a tree (see photo). Spread Mocha Buttercream Frosting over cake roll. Score frosting with fork tines to resemble bark. Garnish, if desired. **Yield:** 8 servings.

Amaretto Filling
½ teaspoon unflavored gelatin
1 tablespoon cold water
1 tablespoon powdered sugar
1 tablespoon cocoa
½ cup whipping cream
1½ teaspoons amaretto

Sprinkle gelatin over cold water in a small saucepan; let stand 1 minute. Cook over low heat, stirring until gelatin dissolves, about 2 minutes. Set aside.

Combine sugar and cocoa; set aside.

Beat whipping cream at low speed of an electric mixer, gradually adding dissolved gelatin. Beat at medium speed until mixture begins to thicken. Add powdered sugar mixture, and beat at high speed until soft peaks form. Stir in amaretto. **Yield:** 1 cup.

Mocha Buttercream Frosting
¼ cup butter or margarine, softened
2½ cups sifted powdered sugar
2½ tablespoons cocoa
2 to 3 tablespoons strongly brewed coffee
1 teaspoon vanilla extract

Beat butter at medium speed of an electric mixer until creamy; add sugar, cocoa, 2 tablespoons coffee (at room temperature), and vanilla, beating until blended. Add enough remaining coffee, if necessary, for spreading consistency. **Yield:** 1¼ cups.

Fast Frost
- Use 1 (16-ounce) can chocolate fudge frosting in place of Mocha Buttercream Frosting. Stir in 1 to 2 tablespoons strongly brewed coffee to add the touch of mocha for Bûche de Noël.

Apple-Cranberry Tarts, page 81

Best-Loved Pies & Pastries

The term "easy as pie" rings proudly on these pages. Let these pies create quick dessert opportunities during the holiday rush. See our primer for ways to interchange commercial crusts with homemade pastries for these recipes. Then experiment with pastry leaves and lattices as you let the artist in you enjoy the season.

Piecrust Primer

A tender, flaky piecrust is the building block for great pies. We give you four choices below, from refrigerated and frozen commercial piecrusts to two homemade versions. You can use any of these options to make pies throughout this chapter. Just keep in mind the variables below.

- *One of our test kitchen staff's best kept secrets is how often they use **refrigerated piecrusts**. Two crusts come in a 15-ounce package. You unfold the crust and fit it in your own pieplate according to package directions. Flute the edges, and your crust will look homemade.*

- *The easiest piecrusts—**frozen piecrusts**—are available in aluminum pans ready for baking. The ones labeled 9-inch crusts are smaller than most 9-inch pieplates. If you use one of these, all of the filling may not fit, and you may need to decrease baking time slightly. Though these crusts are timesavers, they can crack easily; inspect them carefully in the store.*

- *Try our recipe for **Quick-and-Easy Pastry Mix**. One recipe of the mix gives you seven crusts. Store the mix in an airtight container up to one month.*

- *Pastry purists will love our **Classic Pastry** recipe. This version is certain to produce tender, flaky crusts every time.*

Quick-and-Easy Pastry Mix

7 cups all-purpose flour
1 tablespoon salt
2 cups shortening

Combine flour and salt in a large bowl, stirring well with a wire whisk. Cut shortening into flour mixture with a pastry blender until mixture is crumbly.

Store in an airtight container at room temperature up to 1 month. **Yield:** about 9 cups.

For one 9-inch pastry shell, you'll need 3 to 4 tablespoons cold water and 1¼ cups Quick-and-Easy Pastry Mix.

Sprinkle cold water (1 tablespoon at a time) evenly over mix. Stir with a fork just until dry ingredients are moistened. Shape dough into a ball; cover and chill.

Roll dough to ⅛-inch thickness on a lightly floured surface. Place in a 9-inch pieplate; trim off excess pastry around edges. Fold edges under; flute. Bake according to recipe directions.

For baked pastry shell, prick bottom and sides of pastry with a fork. Bake at 425° for 12 to 15 minutes or until golden. **Yield:** one 9-inch pastry shell.

Classic Pastry

1¼ cups all-purpose flour
½ teaspoon salt
⅓ cup plus 2 tablespoons shortening
3 to 4 tablespoons cold water

Combine flour and salt in a small bowl. Cut in shortening with a pastry blender until mixture is crumbly. Sprinkle cold water (1 tablespoon at a time) over surface; stir with a fork just until dry ingredients are moistened. Shape dough into a ball; cover and chill.

Roll dough to ⅛-inch thickness on a lightly floured surface. Place in a 9-inch pieplate; trim off excess pastry along edges. Fold edges under; flute.

For baked pastry shell, prick bottom and sides of pastry generously with a fork. Bake at 450° for 10 to 12 minutes or until golden. **Yield:** one 9-inch pastry shell.

Buttermilk Chess Pie

The Southern Living *staff rarely gives a very easy recipe a perfect rating, but this seven-ingredient pie scored one.*

 5 large eggs, lightly beaten
 2 cups sugar
 ⅔ cup buttermilk
 ½ cup butter or margarine, melted
 2 tablespoons all-purpose flour
 1 teaspoon vanilla extract
 1 unbaked 9-inch pastry shell

Combine first 6 ingredients; stir well. Pour filling into pastry shell.

Bake at 350° for 45 minutes or until set. Let cool on a wire rack. **Yield:** one 9-inch pie.

Coconut-Pecan Chess Pie

 3 large eggs, lightly beaten
 1 cup sugar
 ⅓ cup buttermilk
 2 tablespoons butter or margarine, melted
 1 tablespoon cornmeal
 ½ teaspoon coconut flavoring
 ¾ cup flaked coconut
 ¼ cup chopped pecans
 1 unbaked 9-inch pastry shell

Combine first 6 ingredients; stir in coconut and pecans. Pour filling into pastry shell.

Bake at 400° for 10 minutes. Reduce heat to 350°, and bake 30 additional minutes. Let cool on a wire rack. **Yield:** one 9-inch pie.

Lemon Pie

This is one of the easiest all-occasion dessert recipes you'll find.

 2 medium lemons
 6 large eggs, lightly beaten
 2½ cups sugar
 ¼ cup fresh lemon juice
 ½ cup butter or margarine, melted
 1 unbaked 9-inch pastry shell
   Garnishes: frozen whipped topping (thawed), lemon wedges

Grate rind from lemons; set aside grated rind. Remove and discard pith from lemons. Quarter and seed lemons.

Combine lemon quarters, grated rind, eggs, sugar, and lemon juice in container of an electric blender; cover and process 1 minute or until smooth, stopping once to scrape down sides. Add butter; cover and process 30 seconds. Pour mixture into pastry shell.

Bake at 350° for 40 to 45 minutes or until slightly firm in center. Let cool on a wire rack. Garnish, if desired. **Yield:** one 9-inch pie.

Lemon Pie

Apple-Bourbon Pie

Apple-Bourbon Pie

½ cup raisins
½ cup bourbon
3 pounds cooking apples
¾ cup sugar
2 tablespoons all-purpose flour
1 teaspoon ground cinnamon
¼ teaspoon salt
⅛ teaspoon ground nutmeg
½ cup chopped pecans or walnuts, toasted
1 (15-ounce) package refrigerated piecrusts
2 teaspoons apricot preserves, melted
1 tablespoon buttermilk
1 tablespoon sugar

Combine raisins and bourbon, and let soak at least 2 hours.

Peel apples, and cut into ½-inch slices; arrange apple slices in a steamer basket over boiling water. Cover and steam 10 minutes or until apple slices are tender.

Combine ¾ cup sugar and next 4 ingredients in a large bowl; stir in apple slices, soaked raisins, and pecans.

Fit 1 piecrust into a 9-inch pieplate according to package directions; brush preserves over bottom. Spoon apple mixture into piecrust.

Roll remaining piecrust to press out fold lines; cut with a 3-inch leaf-shaped cutter. Mark veins on leaves with a pastry wheel or sharp knife. Arrange pastry leaves over apple mixture; brush leaves with buttermilk, and sprinkle pie with 1 tablespoon sugar.

Bake at 450° on lower rack of oven 15 minutes. Shield edges of pie with strips of aluminum foil to prevent excessive browning. Bake at 350° for 30 to 35 additional minutes. Let cool on a wire rack. **Yield:** one 9-inch pie.

Pear-Macadamia Pie

Ripe pears make a big difference in this dessert. Plan ahead so the fruit will be ripe when you're ready to bake.

½ (15-ounce) package refrigerated piecrusts
½ cup pear preserves
2 tablespoons Frangelico
⅔ cup macadamia nuts
½ cup sugar
1½ tablespoons all-purpose flour
¼ cup butter or margarine, softened
1 large egg
2½ pounds ripe cooking pears, peeled, cored, and thinly sliced

Unfold piecrust, and lightly roll to fit a 10-inch pieplate. Fit piecrust into pieplate according to package directions. Bake as directed.

Combine preserves and Frangelico in a small heavy saucepan; cook over medium heat, stirring constantly, until warm. Pour mixture through a wire-mesh strainer, discarding solids. Gently brush a thin layer of glaze over warm pastry, reserving remaining glaze.

Position knife blade in food processor bowl; add nuts, sugar, and flour. Process until finely ground. Add butter and egg; process until smooth. Spread mixture evenly over pastry; freeze 15 minutes.

Arrange pear slices over nut mixture; bake at 350° for 30 minutes. Cover loosely with aluminum foil, and bake 40 additional minutes or until pears are tender and golden. Remove from oven; immediately brush pears with reserved glaze. Let cool on a wire rack. **Yield:** one 10-inch pie.

Cranberry-Cherry Pie

Cranberry-Cherry Pie

Two tangy fruits mingle under a flaky pastry of star cutouts. Tapioca is the old-fashioned thickener.

1 (21-ounce) can cherry pie filling
1 (16-ounce) can whole-berry cranberry sauce
¼ cup quick-cooking tapioca
2 tablespoons sugar
1 tablespoon butter, melted
1 teaspoon lemon juice
¼ teaspoon ground cinnamon
Pastry for double-crust 9-inch pie
Milk

Combine first 7 ingredients; stir well. Let stand 15 minutes.

Roll half of pastry to ⅛-inch thickness on a lightly floured surface. Place in a 9-inch pieplate. Spoon cherry mixture into pastry shell.

Roll remaining pastry to ⅛-inch thickness. Using 2½-inch and 1½-inch star cookie cutters, cut out 5 stars. Set cutouts aside. Moisten edges of filled pastry shell with water. Transfer remaining pastry to top of pie. Trim off excess pastry along edges. Fold edges under, and crimp.

Arrange cutouts on top of pie. Brush pastry top and cutouts with milk.

Bake at 400° for 20 minutes. Shield edges of pie with aluminum foil to prevent excessive browning, and bake 20 additional minutes. **Yield:** one 9-inch pie.

Mincemeat Pie

1 (15-ounce) package refrigerated piecrusts
1 teaspoon all-purpose flour
1 (28-ounce) jar prepared mincemeat
1 cup chopped pecans, toasted
2 tablespoons Grand Marnier or orange juice
   Orange Hard Sauce

Unfold 1 piecrust, and press out fold lines; sprinkle with flour, spreading over surface. Place crust, floured side down, in a 9-inch pieplate; set aside.

Combine mincemeat, pecans, and Grand Marnier; spoon mixture into pastry shell.

Roll remaining piecrust to press out fold lines. Cut into ½-inch strips, using a knife or pastry wheel, and arrange in a lattice design over filling. Trim off any excess pastry along the edges. Fold edges under, and crimp.

Bake at 425° for 30 minutes or until golden. Serve warm or cold with Orange Hard Sauce. **Yield:** one 9-inch pie.

Orange Hard Sauce

2 cups sifted powdered sugar
⅔ cup butter or margarine, softened
2 tablespoons Grand Marnier or orange juice

Combine all ingredients; beat at medium speed of an electric mixer until smooth. **Yield:** 1 cup.

Mincemeat Pie with Orange Hard Sauce

Bourbon-Pecan-Pumpkin Pie

Mashed sweet potato would also be a delight in this holiday dessert laced with bourbon.

  3 large eggs, lightly beaten
  1 (16-ounce) can pumpkin
  1 cup half-and-half
  ¾ cup firmly packed dark brown sugar
  3 tablespoons bourbon
  1 teaspoon ground cinnamon
  ½ teaspoon ground ginger
  ¼ teaspoon salt
  1 unbaked 9-inch pastry shell
  2 tablespoons butter or margarine
  ¼ cup firmly packed dark brown sugar
  1 cup chopped pecans, toasted
  2 tablespoons bourbon

Combine first 8 ingredients, stirring until blended. Pour into pastry shell.

Bake at 425° for 10 minutes. Reduce heat to 350°; bake 40 additional minutes or until set. Let cool on a wire rack.

Combine butter and ¼ cup brown sugar in a saucepan; cook over medium heat, stirring until sugar dissolves. Add pecans and 2 tablespoons bourbon, stirring to coat pecans. Spoon mixture over pie. **Yield:** one 9-inch pie.

Rum-Laced Pecan Pie

   1 cup sugar
   1 cup light corn syrup
  ⅓ cup butter or margarine
   4 large eggs, lightly beaten
   3 tablespoons dark rum
   1 teaspoon vanilla extract
  ¼ teaspoon salt
   1 (15-ounce) package refrigerated piecrusts
1¼ cups pecan halves

Combine first 3 ingredients in a medium saucepan; cook over low heat, stirring constantly, until sugar dissolves and butter melts. Remove from heat; let cool slightly. Stir in eggs and next 3 ingredients.

Fit 1 piecrust in a 9-inch pieplate according to package directions. Cut leaf shapes or other desired shapes from remaining piecrust, using cookie cutters. Arrange cutouts around edge of pieplate, pressing gently.

Pour filling into prepared piecrust; top with pecan halves. Bake at 325° for 1 hour and 10 minutes or until pie is set. Let cool on a wire rack. **Yield:** one 9-inch pie.

Sweet Potato Pie with Gingersnap Streusel

Use the thick type of gingersnap cookies when making this recipe.

- 2 cups gingersnap crumbs
- ⅓ cup butter or margarine, melted
- 1 (29-ounce) can sweet potatoes, drained and mashed
- 1¼ cups evaporated milk
- ¾ cup firmly packed brown sugar
- 1¼ teaspoons ground cinnamon
- 1 teaspoon ground allspice
- 3 large eggs, lightly beaten
- ⅔ cup coarsely crushed gingersnaps
- ⅓ cup firmly packed brown sugar
- 3 tablespoons all-purpose flour
- 2 tablespoons butter or margarine, cut up
- Garnish: sweetened whipped cream

Combine 2 cups gingersnap crumbs and ⅓ cup melted butter; stir well. Press crumb mixture into bottom and up sides of a 9½-inch deep-dish pieplate. Bake at 350° for 6 to 8 minutes. Let cool.

Combine sweet potato and next 5 ingredients; stir well with a wire whisk. Pour sweet potato mixture into crust.

Bake at 350° for 20 minutes.

Combine ⅔ cup crushed gingersnaps, ⅓ cup brown sugar, and flour; cut in 2 tablespoons butter with a pastry blender until mixture is crumbly.

Sprinkle streusel over pie, and bake 15 additional minutes. Cover pie with aluminum foil, and bake 25 additional minutes or until set. Let cool on a wire rack. Garnish, if desired. **Yield:** one 9½-inch deep-dish pie.

Sweet Potato Pie with Gingersnap Streusel

Chocolate-Pecan Tassies

Chocolate-Pecan Tassies

Here's an ideal gift—rich chocolate tartlets that are easy to transport. And you can make the pastry in advance and freeze it.

- 2 large eggs, lightly beaten
- ⅔ cup sugar
- ½ cup light corn syrup
- 2 tablespoons plus 2 teaspoons butter or margarine, melted
- ¾ teaspoon vanilla extract
- ¾ cup finely chopped pecans
- ⅓ cup semisweet chocolate mini-morsels
  Chocolate-Cream Cheese Pastry Shells

Combine first 5 ingredients in a large bowl; stir well. Add pecans and mini-morsels; stir well.

Pour mixture into Chocolate-Cream Cheese Pastry Shells. Bake at 350° for 30 minutes or until set. Let cool 5 minutes in muffin pans. Remove from pans; let cool completely on wire racks. **Yield:** 2 dozen.

Chocolate-Cream Cheese Pastry Shells

- ⅓ cup butter or margarine, softened
- 1 (3-ounce) package cream cheese, softened
- ¾ cup plus 1 tablespoon all-purpose flour
- 3 tablespoons cocoa
- 2½ tablespoons powdered sugar

Beat butter and cream cheese at medium speed of an electric mixer until creamy.

Combine flour, cocoa, and powdered sugar; stir well. Gradually add flour mixture to creamed mixture, beating well. Wrap dough in wax paper, and chill 2 hours.

Divide dough into 24 balls. Place in lightly greased 1¾-inch miniature muffin pans, shaping dough to make shells. Prick bottom of each shell with a fork; cover and chill at least 1 hour. **Yield:** 2 dozen pastry shells.

Chocolate-Coconut Pies

You can substitute two frozen 9-inch deep-dish pastry shells here to make cleanup ultra-easy.

1 (15-ounce) package refrigerated piecrusts
2 teaspoons all-purpose flour
1 cup butter or margarine
4 (1-ounce) squares semisweet chocolate
2 cups sugar
½ cup light corn syrup
¼ teaspoon salt
6 large eggs, lightly beaten
1 teaspoon vanilla extract
1 (7-ounce) can flaked coconut

Unfold piecrusts, and press out fold lines; sprinkle each with 1 teaspoon flour, spreading over surface. Place crusts, floured sides down, in 2 (9-inch) pieplates; fold edges under, and crimp.

Combine butter and chocolate in a medium saucepan; cook over low heat until chocolate melts, stirring often. Remove from heat. Add sugar, corn syrup, and salt, stirring well. Let cool slightly.

Stir in eggs, vanilla, and coconut. Pour into prepared pastry shells.

Bake at 350° for 35 minutes or just until set. (Do not overbake.) **Yield:** two 9-inch pies.

Southern Pecan Tartlets

1 tablespoon butter or margarine
1 cup chopped pecans
⅛ teaspoon salt
1 (15-ounce) package refrigerated piecrusts
½ cup butter or margarine
1 cup light corn syrup
1 cup sugar
1 teaspoon vanilla extract
½ teaspoon lemon juice
¼ teaspoon ground cinnamon
3 large eggs, lightly beaten

Place 1 tablespoon butter in a large shallow pan; bake at 350° until melted. Add pecans, stirring to coat; bake 8 to 10 minutes or until toasted, stirring once. Remove from oven, and sprinkle with salt; let cool.

Roll 1 piecrust on a lightly floured surface to press out fold lines. Cut into rounds with a 2½-inch round cutter. Fit pastry rounds into 1¾-inch miniature muffin pans (do not trim edges). Repeat procedure with remaining piecrust. Sprinkle toasted pecans evenly into tart shells; set aside.

Place ½ cup butter in a small heavy saucepan; cook over medium heat, stirring constantly, until lightly browned (do not burn). Remove from heat; let cool 10 minutes.

Add corn syrup and remaining 5 ingredients to butter, stirring well; spoon evenly over pecans in tart shells.

Bake at 350° for 35 to 40 minutes or until set. Let cool in pans 5 minutes. Remove from pans; let cool completely on wire racks. **Yield:** 4½ dozen.

Apple-Cranberry Tarts

1 (15-ounce) package refrigerated piecrusts
2 teaspoons all-purpose flour
4 cups fresh cranberries
1¾ cups peeled, chopped cooking apples
2½ cups sugar
½ cup water
2 tablespoons cornstarch
2 tablespoons water
½ cup chopped pecans
1 tablespoon grated orange rind
1 tablespoon butter, melted
   Sweetened whipped cream

Roll 1 piecrust into a 10-inch circle on a lightly floured surface; sprinkle with 1 teaspoon flour. Cut into 4 (4½-inch) circles. Fit each circle into a 4-inch round tart pan with removable bottom, and place pans on a baking sheet. Prick bottom and sides of crusts with a fork. Repeat procedure with remaining piecrust and 1 teaspoon flour. Reserve remaining pastry for garnish.

Combine cranberries and next 3 ingredients in a saucepan. Bring to a boil; reduce heat, and simmer 10 minutes.

Combine cornstarch and 2 tablespoons water; stir into cranberry mixture, and cook over low heat 2 minutes. Let cool. Stir in pecans and grated orange rind. Spoon into pastry shells.

Bake at 425° for 15 to 20 minutes. Let cool completely on a wire rack.

Cut 32 (3- x ½-inch) strips from reserved pastry, using a fluted pastry wheel. Pinch ends of 16 strips together to resemble loops of a bow. Place loops and remaining strips on an ungreased baking sheet.

Bake at 425° for 10 minutes or until browned. Brush with butter. Let cool.

Place 2 loops and 2 strips on each tart to form a bow. Freeze up to 2 months, if desired; thaw before serving. Pipe with whipped cream. **Yield:** 8 tarts.

Linzer Fudge Tarts

1 (21½-ounce) package fudge brownie mix
½ cup water
½ cup vegetable oil
2 large eggs, lightly beaten
½ teaspoon almond extract
¼ cup raspberry preserves
4 (1-ounce) squares semisweet chocolate, melted and cooled
   Sliced almonds, toasted

Combine first 5 ingredients; stir well. Spoon batter into paper-lined muffin pans, filling two-thirds full. Bake at 350° for 20 minutes or until a wooden pick inserted in center comes out clean. Remove from pans; let cool on wire racks.

Melt preserves in a saucepan over low heat. Make an indentation in the center of each tart, using the handle of a wooden spoon. Spoon ½ teaspoon of melted preserves into each indentation.

Spoon chocolate into a zip-top plastic bag; seal plastic bag. Snip a tiny hole in one corner of bag, using scissors, and pipe chocolate over tarts. Top with almond slices. **Yield:** 1½ dozen.

...Linzer Fudge Tart

Rum-Raisin Fruit Tarts

These raisins plump full of rum as they soak overnight.

- ⅓ cup raisins
- ¼ cup dark rum
- Pastry for 2 double-crust 9-inch pies
- 3 cups peeled, sliced cooking apples
- 1½ teaspoons lemon juice
- ¼ cup sugar
- ¼ cup firmly packed brown sugar
- 2 tablespoons all-purpose flour
- ¼ teaspoon ground cinnamon
- ¼ teaspoon ground nutmeg
- 1 tablespoon butter or margarine

Combine raisins and rum in a small bowl; cover and let stand 8 hours.

Roll half of pastry to ⅛-inch thickness on a lightly floured surface. Cut into 6-inch circles, and place in 6 (4-inch) tart pans with removable sides.

Combine apple slices and lemon juice in a large bowl; set aside. Combine sugars, flour, cinnamon, and nutmeg, stirring well. Spoon over apple mixture, tossing gently. Drain raisins, discarding rum. Add raisins to apple mixture; toss well. Spoon filling evenly into tart shells, and dot with butter.

Line a large baking sheet with parchment paper; set aside. Roll remaining half of pastry to ⅛-inch thickness on a lightly floured surface; cut into ½-inch strips. Arrange strips in a tight weave, lattice fashion, on prepared baking sheet. Chill 1 hour.

Cut into 6 (5-inch) circles, and carefully place one on each tart. Trim off excess pastry along edges; fold edges under, and flute.

Bake at 450° for 10 minutes. Reduce heat to 350°, and bake 10 additional minutes or until golden. Let cool completely. **Yield:** ½ dozen.

Rum-Raisin Fruit Tarts

Cranberry-Walnut Tart

1½ cups all-purpose flour
1   cup chopped walnuts
¼   cup sugar
½   cup butter or margarine
1   large egg, lightly beaten
1   teaspoon vanilla extract
1   envelope unflavored gelatin
¼   cup cold water
3   cups fresh cranberries
1   cup sugar
½   cup red currant jelly
½   cup whipping cream, whipped

Combine first 3 ingredients in a medium mixing bowl; cut in butter with a pastry blender until mixture is crumbly. Add egg and vanilla; stir with a fork until dry ingredients are moistened. Press mixture on bottom and 1¼ inches up sides of a lightly greased 9-inch spring-form pan.

Bake at 350° for 15 to 20 minutes or until golden. Let cool completely.

Sprinkle gelatin over cold water in a small bowl; set aside. Combine cranberries, 1 cup sugar, and jelly in a saucepan; cook over low heat 10 minutes or until cranberry skins pop. Remove from heat; let cool 5 minutes.

Add softened gelatin; stir until dissolved. Let cool completely.

Pour cranberry mixture into tart shell. Chill. Place tart on a platter, and remove sides of pan before serving. Pipe whipped cream on top of tart. **Yield:** one 9-inch tart.

Hazelnut Pumpkin Tart

Hazelnut Pumpkin Tart

You can find a jar of crystallized ginger in the spice section at the supermarket.

- 1 (15-ounce) package refrigerated piecrusts
- 1 cup hazelnuts, toasted, skinned, and finely chopped
- 3 large eggs
- 1 (16-ounce) can pumpkin
- 1 cup half-and-half
- ½ cup firmly packed brown sugar
- ⅓ cup sugar
- ¾ teaspoon ground ginger
- ¾ teaspoon ground cinnamon
- ¼ teaspoon ground allspice
- ⅛ teaspoon salt
- 1 cup whipping cream
- ½ cup sifted powdered sugar
- 1 tablespoon minced crystallized ginger
- 30 whole hazelnuts, toasted and skinned

Roll 1 piecrust into a 12-inch circle on a floured surface. Fit into an 11-inch tart pan with removable bottom. Prick bottom and sides of pastry. Bake at 375° for 5 minutes. Let cool in pan on a wire rack. Sprinkle with chopped hazelnuts.

Beat eggs at high speed of an electric mixer; add pumpkin and next 7 ingredients, beating well. Pour into prepared pastry. Bake at 375° for 35 minutes or until set. Let cool in pan on wire rack. Cover and chill at least 2 hours.

Cut 30 shapes from remaining piecrust, using a leaf cookie cutter. Reserve any remaining piecrust for another use. Place leaves on an ungreased baking sheet. Bake at 450° for 6 minutes. Remove to wire rack; let cool.

Beat whipping cream until foamy; gradually add powdered sugar, beating until soft peaks form. Fold in crystallized ginger. Cover and chill 1 hour. Arrange whole hazelnuts and pastry leaves on tart. Serve with whipped cream mixture. **Yield:** one 11-inch tart.

White Chocolate Chess Tart

There's just enough white chocolate in this tart to create a creamy, buttery unforgettable dessert. A thin slice is an indulgence.

- ½ (15-ounce) package refrigerated piecrusts
- 4 ounces white chocolate, chopped
- ½ cup buttermilk
- 3 large eggs, lightly beaten
- 1 tablespoon vanilla extract
- 1¼ cups sugar
- 3 tablespoons all-purpose flour
- 1 tablespoon cornmeal
  Pinch of salt

Fit 1 piecrust into a 9-inch tart pan with removable bottom according to package directions; trim edges. Line pastry with aluminum foil, and fill with pie weights or dried beans.

Bake at 450° for 8 minutes. Remove weights and foil; bake 3 to 4 additional minutes. Let cool on a wire rack.

Combine chocolate and buttermilk in a saucepan; cook over low heat, stirring constantly, until chocolate melts and mixture is smooth. Let cool 15 minutes.

Combine eggs and vanilla; gradually stir in chocolate mixture. Combine sugar and remaining 3 ingredients; gradually add to chocolate mixture, stirring until blended. Pour into piecrust.

Bake at 325° for 50 minutes or until a knife inserted in center comes out clean. Let cool on a wire rack. **Yield:** one 9-inch tart.

Toasting Hazelnuts

- *The most common way to buy hazelnuts is whole, with their cinnamon-brown skins intact.*
- *The easiest way to toast hazelnuts and to remove their skins is to spread whole nuts in an ungreased jellyroll pan. Bake at 350° for 12 to 15 minutes. The skins will begin to split. Using a hot pad, scoop hot nuts into a colander. Cover with a kitchen towel, and let sit 1 minute. Rub nuts briskly in towel to remove skins.*

Hot Cranberry Bake

4 cups peeled, chopped cooking apples
2 cups fresh cranberries
1½ teaspoons lemon juice
1 cup sugar
1⅓ cups quick-cooking oats, uncooked
1 cup chopped walnuts
⅓ cup firmly packed brown sugar
½ cup butter or margarine, melted
  Vanilla ice cream

Combine apple and cranberries in a lightly greased 2-quart baking dish. Sprinkle with lemon juice; top with sugar.

Combine oats, walnuts, brown sugar, and butter. Stir mixture just until dry ingredients are moistened and mixture is crumbly. Sprinkle over fruit.

Bake at 325° for 1 hour. Serve warm with vanilla ice cream. **Yield:** 8 servings.

Apple Strudel

Keep unused sheets of puff pastry covered with a damp cloth to prevent them from drying out.

1 (17¼-ounce) package commercial frozen puff pastry sheets, thawed
2 tablespoons butter or margarine, melted and divided
¼ cup firmly packed brown sugar
1 teaspoon grated lemon rind
½ cup chopped pecans, divided
½ cup raisins, divided
1 (21-ounce) can apple pie filling, chopped

Roll each sheet of pastry into a 12- x 9-inch rectangle on a lightly floured surface. Brush a rectangle with 1 tablespoon melted butter. Combine brown sugar and lemon rind; sprinkle half of brown sugar mixture on buttered pastry.

Sprinkle half of chopped pecans and raisins over brown sugar mixture. Brush remaining 1 tablespoon melted butter over second sheet of pastry. Place second sheet on top of first sheet, buttered side up. Sprinkle with remaining brown sugar mixture, chopped pecans, and raisins.

Spoon pie filling down 1 (12-inch) edge of pastry; starting with long side, roll up, jellyroll fashion. Place strudel, seam side down, on a lightly greased baking sheet. With a knife, make diagonal 2-inch slits in top of pastry every 1 to 2 inches.

Bake at 400° for 40 minutes or until golden. **Yield:** one 12-inch strudel.

Hot Cranberry Bake

Apple Dumplings with Maple-Cider Sauce

- 3 cups all-purpose flour
- 1 teaspoon salt
- ¾ cup butter or margarine, chilled and cut into pieces
- ¼ cup plus 1 tablespoon shortening
- ½ cup apple cider, chilled
- 8 large Granny Smith apples
- ½ cup firmly packed brown sugar
- ½ cup currants
- ½ cup chopped walnuts
- ⅓ cup butter or margarine, softened
- 1 large egg
- 1 tablespoon water
- 4 (3-inch) sticks cinnamon, broken in half
  Maple-Cider Sauce

Combine flour and salt; cut in chilled butter and shortening with a pastry blender until mixture is crumbly. Sprinkle cider, 1 tablespoon at a time, evenly over top; stir with a fork until dry ingredients are moistened. Shape into 2 (½-inch-thick) squares; cover and chill.

Core each apple, leaving ½ inch intact on bottom. Peel top two-thirds of each apple; set apples aside.

Combine sugar, currants, and walnuts; stir in softened butter, blending well. Spoon evenly into each apple.

Roll pastry squares to ⅛-inch thickness on a floured surface; cut each square into 4 (7-inch) squares.

Press 1 pastry square around each apple; remove excess pastry from bottom so apple will sit level. Reroll pastry scraps, if desired; cut into leaf shapes.

Combine egg and water, beating lightly with a fork. Brush over apples, and attach leaf shapes, if desired.

Place a cinnamon stick half in top of each apple to resemble a stem. Place

Apple Dumpling with Maple-Cider Sauce

apples in a lightly greased 15- x 10- x 1-inch jellyroll pan.

Bake at 375° for 40 minutes. Pour Maple-Cider Sauce over apples; bake 15 additional minutes or until apples are tender. Place apples on a serving plate, and spoon sauce around apples. **Yield:** 8 servings.

Note: Serve maple whipped cream with the apples, if desired. To make it, combine 1 cup whipping cream and 3 tablespoons maple syrup in a medium bowl. Beat at high speed of an electric mixer until soft peaks form.

Maple-Cider Sauce

- 2 teaspoons cornstarch
- 1½ cups apple cider
- ⅔ cup maple syrup
- ¼ cup firmly packed brown sugar
- ¼ cup fresh lemon juice

Combine cornstarch and cider in a saucepan, stirring until smooth; add maple syrup and remaining ingredients. Bring to a boil over medium-high heat; boil 1 minute. **Yield:** 2 cups.

Candy Cane Bread, page 106

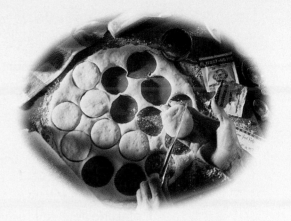

Christmas Breads

Deck the halls with fresh-baked breads…like our banana nut bread, garlic bread, or cornbread. Send favorite aromas dancing through your senses with flaky biscuits, scones, and streusel-topped muffins. This all-occasion selection of the staff of life will fill any basket with Christmas spirit.

Cloud Biscuits

Stir these six ingredients together to get a biscuit that's as light as a cloud.

- 2¼ cups self-rising flour
- 1 tablespoon sugar
- ½ cup butter-flavored shortening
- 1 large egg, lightly beaten
- ⅔ cup milk
- 1 tablespoon butter or margarine, melted

Combine flour and sugar in a medium bowl, stirring well. Cut in shortening with a pastry blender until mixture is crumbly.

Combine egg and milk; add to flour mixture, stirring just until dry ingredients are moistened. Turn dough out onto a floured surface; knead 3 or 4 times.

Roll dough to ½-inch thickness; cut with a 3-inch biscuit cutter. Place biscuits on an ungreased baking sheet.

Bake at 450° for 10 to 12 minutes or until biscuits are golden. Remove from oven; brush hot biscuits with butter. **Yield:** 1 dozen.

Cloud Biscuits

Easy Herb Biscuits

Try using your favorite two herbs in place of the chives and parsley—the combinations are endless.

- 2 cups biscuit mix
- 1 tablespoon freeze-dried chives
- 1 teaspoon dried parsley flakes
- ¾ cup plain yogurt

Combine all ingredients in a medium bowl, stirring just until dry ingredients are moistened. Turn dough out onto a floured surface, and knead 4 or 5 times.

Roll dough to ½-inch thickness; cut with a 2-inch biscuit cutter. Place biscuits on a lightly greased baking sheet.

Bake at 450° for 8 minutes or until lightly browned. **Yield:** 1 dozen.

Sweet Little Biscuits

This recipe has just enough sugar to qualify it as dessert. Top the biscuits off with a drizzle of honey or syrup.

- 3 cups all-purpose flour
- 1 tablespoon baking powder
- ½ teaspoon baking soda
- ½ teaspoon salt
- ⅓ cup sugar
- ¾ cup butter or margarine
- 1 cup buttermilk
  Milk

Combine first 5 ingredients, stirring well; cut in butter with a pastry blender until mixture is crumbly. Add buttermilk, stirring until dry ingredients are moistened. Shape dough into a ball, and knead 4 or 5 times.

Roll dough to ½-inch thickness on a lightly floured surface. Cut with a 1¾-inch biscuit cutter, and place biscuits on ungreased baking sheets. Brush biscuits lightly with milk.

Bake at 400° for 12 to 15 minutes or until lightly browned. **Yield:** 3 dozen.

Whipping Cream Biscuits

Whipping cream is the ultimate ingredient when you want fluffy biscuits.

- 2 cups all-purpose flour
- 1 tablespoon plus 1 teaspoon baking powder
- ¼ teaspoon salt
- 1 tablespoon sugar
- ¼ cup unsalted butter
- 1 cup plus 1 tablespoon whipping cream

Combine first 4 ingredients in a medium bowl; cut in butter with a pastry blender until mixture is crumbly. Add whipping cream, stirring just until dry ingredients are moistened. Turn dough out onto a lightly floured surface, and knead 5 or 6 times.

Roll dough to ½-inch thickness; cut with a 2½-inch biscuit cutter. Place on a lightly greased baking sheet.

Bake at 425° for 10 to 12 minutes or until golden. **Yield:** 10 biscuits.

Gingerbread Scones

In this recipe, four spices mix with molasses and will fill your kitchen with heart-warming holiday aromas.

- 2¼ cups all-purpose flour
- 1 teaspoon baking powder
- ¼ teaspoon baking soda
- 1 teaspoon ground cinnamon
- ½ teaspoon ground ginger
- ¼ teaspoon ground allspice
- ¼ teaspoon ground nutmeg
- ½ cup butter or margarine
- ½ cup currants
- ⅓ cup molasses
- ¾ cup whipping cream
  Lemon Butter

Combine first 7 ingredients; cut in butter with a pastry blender until mixture is crumbly. Stir in currants. Add molasses and whipping cream, stirring just until dry ingredients are moistened. Turn dough out onto a lightly floured surface, and knead 4 or 5 times.

Roll dough to ½-inch thickness on a lightly floured surface; cut with a 2-inch biscuit cutter. Place on a lightly greased baking sheet.

Bake at 425° for 8 to 10 minutes or until lightly browned. Serve with Lemon Butter. **Yield:** 2 dozen.

Lemon Butter
- ¼ cup butter or margarine, softened
- ¼ cup sifted powdered sugar
- 1 teaspoon grated lemon rind
- 1 tablespoon lemon juice

Combine all ingredients, stirring until blended. **Yield:** ⅓ cup.

Perfect Biscuits

The art of making biscuits is easy to master, once you put in place these basic rules:

- *Butter should be cold when you cut it into dry ingredients. This helps produce tender, flaky biscuits.*

- *If you don't own a pastry blender, use a fork and knife or two knives. You'll get the same results.*

- *Once you've added liquid ingredients to dry ones, keep the stirring to a minimum. You want a soft dough. Overstirring toughens biscuits.*

- *Use minimal flour on the work surface when you're rolling and cutting dough. Using too much flour in the dough makes dry biscuits.*

- *If you've misplaced your biscuit cutter, don't worry. Just use the rim of a drinking glass.*

Hazelnut Scones

2 cups all-purpose flour
2 teaspoons baking powder
¼ teaspoon salt
½ cup sugar
⅓ cup butter
½ cup chopped blanched hazelnuts
2 large eggs, lightly beaten
½ cup whipping cream
1½ tablespoons Frangelico
1 tablespoon sugar
18 whole hazelnuts

Combine first 4 ingredients in a large bowl; cut in butter with a pastry blender until mixture is crumbly. Stir in chopped hazelnuts. Make a well in center of mixture. Combine eggs, whipping cream, and Frangelico; add to dry ingredients, stirring just until moistened.

Roll dough to ¾-inch thickness on a lightly floured surface. Cut with a 2½-inch biscuit cutter, and place on lightly greased baking sheets. Sprinkle tops evenly with 1 tablespoon sugar, and place a whole hazelnut in each center.

Bake at 350° for 15 minutes. Serve with honey, butter, or strawberry jam.
Yield: 1½ dozen.

Maple-Pecan Scones with Cinnamon Butter

¾ cup chopped pecans
2¼ cups all-purpose flour
1 teaspoon baking powder
¼ teaspoon baking soda
¼ teaspoon salt
⅓ cup maple-flavored syrup
¾ cup whipping cream
Cinnamon Butter

Spread pecans in a shallow pan. Bake at 350° for 5 minutes.

Position knife blade in food processor bowl; add ⅓ cup pecans. Process pecans until ground (about 5 seconds). Combine ground pecans, remaining chopped pecans, flour, and next 3 ingredients. Add syrup and cream, stirring until dry ingredients are moistened.

Turn dough out onto a lightly floured surface, and knead 4 or 5 times. Pat dough into a 10-inch circle on a greased baking sheet. Using a sharp knife, make 8 shallow cuts in dough, forming wedges.

Bake at 425° for 10 to 12 minutes or until lightly browned. Serve warm with Cinnamon Butter. **Yield:** 8 servings.

Cinnamon Butter
⅓ cup butter, softened
¼ cup maple-flavored syrup
¼ teaspoon ground cinnamon

Beat butter at medium speed of an electric mixer until fluffy; gradually add syrup and cinnamon, beating well.
Yield: about ½ cup.

The Scoop on Scones

• Scones, like biscuits, are loved for their tenderness. The main difference between biscuits and scones is shape. Scones are usually cut into wedges before baking.

• The rules that apply to biscuits about minimal stirring, handling, and additional flour apply here, too.

• Scone dough is typically a bit sticky. Just pat the dough into a rough mound for baking.

Blueberry-Almond Streusel Muffins

¼ cup all-purpose flour
¼ cup sugar
2 tablespoons butter, cut into pieces
¼ cup plus 2 tablespoons chopped almonds
2 cups all-purpose flour
1 tablespoon baking powder
½ teaspoon salt
⅔ cup sugar
2 teaspoons grated lemon rind
1½ cups fresh or frozen blueberries, thawed
2 large eggs, lightly beaten
½ cup milk
½ cup butter, melted and cooled

Combine ¼ cup flour and ¼ cup sugar in a medium bowl. Cut in 2 tablespoons butter with a pastry blender until mixture is crumbly. Stir in almonds. Set almond streusel mixture aside.

Combine 2 cups flour and next 4 ingredients in a large bowl. Add blueberries, and toss gently. Make a well in center of mixture.

Combine eggs, milk, and ½ cup butter; add to dry ingredients, stirring just until dry ingredients are moistened.

Spoon batter into greased muffin pans, filling two-thirds full. Sprinkle evenly with almond streusel mixture.

Bake at 400° for 15 to 20 minutes or until golden. Remove from pans immediately. **Yield:** 16 muffins.

Blueberry-Almond Streusel Muffins

Cranberry-Walnut Streusel Muffins

2 cups all-purpose flour, divided
1 cup firmly packed brown sugar
½ cup butter or margarine
⅔ cup chopped walnuts, divided
2 teaspoons baking powder
½ teaspoon baking soda
½ teaspoon salt
1 teaspoon ground nutmeg
½ teaspoon grated orange rind
2 large eggs, lightly beaten
⅔ cup buttermilk
1 cup fresh cranberries

Combine 1 cup flour and sugar; cut in butter with a pastry blender until mixture is crumbly. Set aside ½ cup flour mixture; stir in 3 tablespoons walnuts. (This will become the streusel topping.)

Combine remaining flour mixture, remaining 1 cup flour, baking powder, and next 4 ingredients in a large bowl. Make a well in center of mixture. Combine eggs and buttermilk. Add to flour mixture, stirring just until moistened. Stir in cranberries and remaining walnuts.

Spoon batter into greased muffin pans, filling half full. Sprinkle evenly with reserved walnut streusel mixture.

Bake at 350° for 20 to 25 minutes. Remove from pans immediately. **Yield:** 1½ dozen.

Banana-Coconut Muffins

2 cups all-purpose flour
1 tablespoon baking powder
½ teaspoon salt
⅓ cup sugar
1 large egg, lightly beaten
1 cup mashed ripe banana
⅔ cup milk
½ cup butter or margarine, melted and cooled
1 teaspoon vanilla extract
1 cup flaked coconut, lightly toasted

Combine first 4 ingredients in a medium bowl; make a well in center of mixture.

Combine egg and next 4 ingredients; stir well. Add coconut; stir just until blended.

Add banana mixture to dry ingredients, stirring just until dry ingredients are moistened. Spoon batter into greased muffin pans, filling two-thirds full.

Bake at 400° for 20 minutes or until golden. Let cool on a wire rack 5 minutes, and remove from pans. **Yield:** 1 dozen.

Banana Pudding Bread

Vanilla wafers are the secret ingredient that gives texture and sweetness to this familiar breakfast bread.

½ cup butter or margarine, softened
¾ cup sugar
2 large eggs
2 cups all-purpose flour
2 teaspoons baking powder
½ teaspoon salt
30 vanilla wafers, finely crushed
1 cup mashed ripe banana
½ cup milk
1 cup chopped walnuts, divided

Beat butter at medium speed of an electric mixer until creamy; gradually add sugar, beating well. Add eggs, one at a time, beating after each addition.

Combine flour and next 3 ingredients; add to creamed mixture alternately with banana and milk, beginning and ending with flour mixture. Mix at low speed after each addition. Stir in ¾ cup walnuts. Spoon batter into a greased and floured 9- x 5- x 3-inch loafpan. Sprinkle with remaining walnuts.

Bake at 350° for 55 minutes to 1 hour or until a wooden pick inserted in center comes out clean, loosely covering with foil after 45 minutes. Let cool in pan on a wire rack 10 minutes; remove from pan, and let cool completely on wire rack. **Yield:** 1 loaf.

Pecan Spice Loaf

½ cup butter, softened
¾ cup firmly packed brown sugar
1 large egg
½ cup molasses
1 tablespoon grated orange rind
2 cups all-purpose flour
2 teaspoons baking powder
½ teaspoon baking soda
1½ teaspoons ground ginger
½ teaspoon ground nutmeg
¼ teaspoon ground cloves
1 cup chopped pecans
¾ cup orange juice

Beat butter in a large bowl at medium speed of an electric mixer until creamy; gradually add brown sugar, beating well. Add egg, beating well. Stir in molasses and orange rind.

Combine flour and next 6 ingredients; add to creamed mixture alternately with juice, beginning and ending with flour mixture. Mix after each addition. Pour batter into a greased and floured 9- x 5- x 3-inch loafpan.

Bake at 350° for 55 minutes or until a wooden pick inserted in center of loaf comes out clean. Let cool in pan 5 minutes; remove from pan, and let cool completely on a wire rack. **Yield:** 1 loaf.

Pumpkin Bread with Cream Cheese and Peach Preserves

2   cups sugar
¾   cup vegetable oil
4   large eggs
1   (16-ounce) can pumpkin
3⅓ cups all-purpose flour
2   teaspoons baking soda
½   teaspoon baking powder
1   teaspoon salt
1   tablespoon pumpkin pie spice
⅔   cup water
2   teaspoons vanilla extract
1   cup chopped pecans
    Cream Cheese and Peach
    Preserves

Combine sugar and oil in a large bowl, stirring well. Add eggs, one at a time, mixing well after each addition. Stir in pumpkin.

Combine flour and next 4 ingredients; add to pumpkin mixture alternately with water, beginning and ending with flour mixture. Stir in vanilla and pecans. Spoon batter into 2 lightly greased 9- x 5- x 3-inch loafpans.

Bake at 325° for 1 hour and 10 to 20 minutes or until a wooden pick inserted in center comes out clean. Let cool in pans 10 minutes; remove from pans, and cool on wire racks. Serve with Cream Cheese and Peach Preserves. **Yield:** 2 loaves.

Cream Cheese and Peach Preserves

¼   cup peach preserves
¼   teaspoon ground ginger
1   (8-ounce) package cream cheese, softened

Combine preserves and ginger; spoon over block of cream cheese. **Yield:** 1 cup.

Holiday Nut Bread

2   large eggs, lightly beaten
½   cup butter or margarine, melted
1   cup mashed ripe banana
1   teaspoon vanilla extract
1½ cups all-purpose flour
1   teaspoon baking soda
1   cup sugar
½   cup chopped pecans
¼   cup flaked coconut
¼   cup raisins

Combine first 4 ingredients in a large bowl. Combine flour, soda, and sugar; add to butter mixture, stirring just until moistened. Fold in pecans, coconut, and raisins. Pour batter into a greased and floured 8½- x 4½- x 3-inch loafpan.

Bake at 350° for 1 hour or until a wooden pick inserted in center of loaf comes out clean. Let cool in pan 10 minutes; remove from pan, and let cool completely on a wire rack. **Yield:** 1 loaf.

Holiday Nut Bread

Pecan Coffee Cake, page 100

Gingerbread Scones, page 91

Bacon-Cheddar Corn Loaf

Use canned mexicorn (11-ounce can, undrained) instead of cream-style corn to spice up this loaf, which makes a great partner for chili.

½ pound bacon
1½ cups all-purpose flour
½ cup yellow cornmeal
2 teaspoons baking powder
½ teaspoon salt
1½ cups (6 ounces) finely shredded Cheddar cheese
1 cup canned cream-style corn
¾ cup milk
½ cup sliced green onions
¼ cup butter or margarine, melted and cooled
2 large eggs, lightly beaten

Cook bacon in a large skillet until crisp; remove bacon, reserving 2 tablespoons drippings. Crumble bacon, and set aside.

Combine flour and next 3 ingredients in a large bowl; make a well in center of mixture. Combine bacon, reserved drippings, cheese, and remaining 5 ingredients; add to dry ingredients, stirring just until dry ingredients are moistened. Spoon batter into a greased and floured 9- x 5- x 3-inch loafpan.

Bake at 350° for 1 hour or until a wooden pick inserted in center comes out clean. Let cool in pan 10 minutes; remove from pan, and let cool completely on a wire rack, if desired. **Yield:** 1 loaf.

Broccoli Cornbread

Broccoli Cornbread

Broccoli, Cheddar cheese, and spicy seasonings distinguish this cornbread from more traditional versions.

1 (10-ounce) package frozen chopped broccoli, thawed
1 (8½-ounce) package cornbread mix
1 cup (4 ounces) shredded Cheddar cheese
½ cup butter or margarine, melted
½ teaspoon salt
½ teaspoon garlic powder
¼ teaspoon ground red pepper
3 large eggs, lightly beaten
1 medium onion, chopped

Press broccoli between paper towels to remove excess moisture. Combine cornbread mix and remaining 7 ingredients; stir well. Stir in broccoli (batter will be thick). Pour mixture into a greased 8-inch square pan.

Bake at 375° for 25 to 30 minutes or until golden. Let cool slightly, and cut into squares. **Yield:** 9 servings.

Bacon Monkey Bread

Canned biscuits make this savory pull-apart bread convenient.

- 11 slices bacon, cooked and crumbled
- ½ cup grated Parmesan cheese
- 1 small onion, chopped
- 3 (10-ounce) cans refrigerated buttermilk biscuits
- ½ cup butter or margarine, melted

Combine first 3 ingredients; set aside.

Cut biscuits into fourths. Dip each piece in butter, and layer one-third in a lightly greased 10-inch Bundt pan.

Sprinkle half of bacon mixture over biscuits; repeat layering procedure, ending with biscuits.

Bake at 350° for 40 minutes or until golden. Let cool in pan 10 minutes; invert onto a serving platter, and serve immediately. **Yield:** one 10-inch ring.

Quick Garlic Bread

- ¼ cup butter or margarine, softened
- 1 tablespoon grated Parmesan cheese
- 1½ teaspoons mayonnaise or salad dressing
- ⅛ teaspoon garlic powder
- ⅛ teaspoon paprika
- 1 (16-ounce) loaf sliced French bread

Combine first 5 ingredients; spread on 1 side of each bread slice. Place on an ungreased baking sheet.

Broil 4 inches from heat (with electric oven door partially opened) 4 to 5 minutes. **Yield:** 1 loaf.

Sausage-Stuffed French Loaf

Use spicy sausage if you prefer bold flavors.

- 1 (16-ounce) loaf French bread
- ½ pound ground pork sausage
- ½ pound lean ground beef
- 1 medium onion, chopped
- 1 cup (4 ounces) shredded mozzarella cheese
- ¼ cup chopped fresh parsley
- 1 teaspoon Dijon mustard
- ¼ teaspoon fennel seeds
- ¼ teaspoon salt
- ¼ teaspoon pepper
- 1 large egg, lightly beaten
- 2 tablespoons butter or margarine
- 1 clove garlic, crushed

Cut off ends of French bread loaf, and set ends aside. Hollow out the center of loaf with a long serrated bread knife, leaving a ½-inch-thick shell. Position knife blade in food processor bowl; add bread removed from inside the loaf. Process to make coarse crumbs. Set bread shell and crumbs aside.

Cook sausage, ground beef, and onion in a skillet until meat is browned, stirring until meat crumbles; drain well. Stir in 1 cup reserved breadcrumbs, cheese, and next 6 ingredients. Spoon meat mixture into bread shell, and replace loaf ends, securing with wooden picks.

Melt butter in a small saucepan; add garlic, and cook about 1 minute. Brush over loaf. Wrap loaf in aluminum foil, leaving open slightly on top.

Bake at 400° for 20 minutes or until cheese thoroughly melts. Cut into 4 pieces. **Yield:** 4 servings.

Orange Bread

Pecan Coffee Cake

3 cups biscuit mix
¼ cup sugar
½ cup milk
¼ cup butter or margarine, melted
1 (8-ounce) package cream cheese, softened
½ cup sugar
½ teaspoon vanilla extract
¼ teaspoon butter flavoring
2 large eggs
  Brown Sugar Glaze
  Pecan halves, toasted

Combine first 4 ingredients in a mixing bowl; stir vigorously until blended. Turn dough out onto a lightly floured surface, and knead 4 or 5 times. Press into bottom and up sides of an ungreased 9-inch round cakepan.

Combine cream cheese and next 4 ingredients in a mixing bowl; beat at medium speed of an electric mixer until smooth. Pour mixture over dough.

Bake at 350° for 35 to 40 minutes or until center is set. Let cool in pan 15 minutes. Spoon Brown Sugar Glaze over top, and arrange pecan halves over edge of glaze. Serve warm or at room temperature. **Yield:** 8 servings.

Brown Sugar Glaze

2 tablespoons firmly packed brown sugar
2 tablespoons butter or margarine
1 tablespoon milk

Combine all ingredients in a small saucepan; bring to a boil over medium heat; cook, stirring constantly, 2 minutes. Remove from heat; let cool to lukewarm. **Yield:** about ¼ cup.

Orange Bread

¾ cup sugar
½ cup chopped pecans
1 tablespoon grated orange rind
2 (11-ounce) cans refrigerated buttermilk biscuits
1 (3-ounce) package cream cheese, cut into 20 squares
½ cup butter or margarine, melted
1 cup sifted powdered sugar
2 to 3 tablespoons orange juice

Combine first 3 ingredients in a small bowl; set aside.

Separate biscuit dough into individual biscuits; gently separate individual biscuits in half. Place a cream cheese square between 2 halves, and pinch sides to seal each back together. Dip in butter, and dredge in reserved sugar mixture. Stand biscuits on edge in a lightly greased 12-cup Bundt pan, spacing evenly.

Drizzle with remaining butter, and sprinkle with remaining sugar mixture.

Bake at 350° for 45 minutes or until golden. Immediately invert onto a serving plate.

Combine powdered sugar and orange juice; stir well. Drizzle over warm bread. Serve immediately. **Yield:** one 10-inch coffee cake.

Raspberry Coffee Cake

2¼ cups all-purpose flour
¾ cup sugar
¾ cup butter or margarine
½ teaspoon baking powder
½ teaspoon baking soda
1 teaspoon almond extract
¾ cup sour cream
3 large eggs, divided
1 (8-ounce) package cream cheese, softened
¼ cup sugar
⅓ cup seedless raspberry preserves
½ cup sliced almonds

Combine flour and ¾ cup sugar; cut in butter with pastry blender until mixture is crumbly. Reserve 1 cup mixture.

Add baking powder, soda, almond extract, sour cream, and 1 egg to remaining flour mixture, stirring well. Firmly press mixture evenly onto bottom and 2 inches up sides of a greased 10-inch springform pan.

Combine remaining 2 eggs, cream cheese, and ¼ cup sugar. Beat at medium speed of an electric mixer until blended. Spoon into crust. Carefully spoon preserves over filling.

Combine reserved 1 cup flour mixture and almonds; sprinkle over preserves.

Bake at 350° for 45 to 50 minutes or until center is set. Let cool 15 minutes on a wire rack; remove sides of pan, and let cool completely. **Yield:** one 10-inch coffee cake.

Raspberry Coffee Cake

Whipping Cream Waffles

2 large eggs, separated
1 cup whipping cream, whipped
1 tablespoon butter or margarine, melted
⅔ cup all-purpose flour
1 teaspoon baking powder
⅛ teaspoon salt
⅓ cup sugar
   Cranberry Butter
   Applesauce Cream

Beat egg yolks in a bowl until thick and pale; fold in whipped cream and butter. Combine flour and next 3 ingredients; fold into whipped cream mixture.

Beat egg whites at high speed of an electric mixer until stiff peaks form; fold into batter (batter will be thick). Spoon half of batter onto a preheated, oiled waffle iron, spreading to edges.

Bake until lightly browned and crisp. Repeat procedure. Serve with Cranberry Butter, Applesauce Cream, syrup, or honey. **Yield:** 2 (8-inch) waffles.

Cranberry Butter
½ cup butter, softened
¼ cup sifted powdered sugar
2 tablespoons whole-berry cranberry sauce

Combine butter and powdered sugar; beat at medium speed of an electric mixer until blended. Stir in cranberry sauce. Spoon mixture into a butter crock; cover and chill. **Yield:** ⅔ cup.

Applesauce Cream
½ cup whipping cream
½ cup applesauce
¼ cup sifted powdered sugar
1 tablespoon lemon juice

Beat whipping cream at medium speed of an electric mixer until soft peaks form; fold in applesauce, powdered sugar, and lemon juice. Cover and chill. **Yield:** 1½ cups.

Crusty Herbed Popovers

If you choose fresh herbs for this recipe, use three times the amount listed for dried.

   Vegetable cooking spray or vegetable oil
2 tablespoons grated Parmesan cheese
1 cup bread flour
1 cup milk
1 tablespoon butter or margarine, melted
1 teaspoon dried thyme
1 teaspoon Worcestershire sauce
¾ teaspoon dried oregano
½ teaspoon salt
¼ teaspoon garlic powder
2 large eggs, lightly beaten
2 egg whites

Grease a popover pan with cooking spray or oil; dust bottom and sides of pan with Parmesan. Set pan aside.

Combine flour and remaining ingredients; stir with a wire whisk until blended. Fill prepared pan three-fourths full. Place in a cold oven. Turn oven on 450°, and bake 15 minutes. Reduce heat to 350°, and bake 35 to 40 additional minutes or until crusty and browned. Serve immediately. **Yield:** 6 popovers.

Crusty Herbed Popover

Tavern Bread

Peel labels from four 16-ounce cans, and sterilize the cans in your dishwasher for use in this recipe.

1	teaspoon instant coffee granules
½	cup water
3	tablespoons molasses
1	tablespoon honey
1	package dry yeast
1	(12-ounce) can evaporated milk
2	tablespoons regular oats, uncooked
2	tablespoons vegetable oil
2	teaspoons salt
¼	teaspoon ground ginger
1½	cups whole wheat flour
3	cups all-purpose flour, divided

Combine first 4 ingredients in a heavy saucepan; cook over low heat until granules dissolve. Let cool to 105° to 115°; transfer to a large mixing bowl. Stir in yeast; let stand 5 minutes. Add milk and next 4 ingredients. Stir in whole wheat flour and 1 cup all-purpose flour.

Beat at medium speed of an electric mixer 1 minute. Gradually add remaining 2 cups all-purpose flour, stirring with a wooden spoon.

Divide dough into 4 well-greased 16-ounce cans. Let rise, uncovered, in a warm place (85°), free from drafts, 1 hour or until doubled in bulk.

Bake at 350° for 30 minutes. Remove from cans immediately, and let cool on wire racks. **Yield:** 4 loaves.

Tavern Bread

Fancy Floss

- Unflavored dental floss has added value when you use it instead of a knife to slice soft dough. Just place floss under dough; then gently, but firmly, pull floss in opposite directions to cut slices from the roll cleanly. (See photo.)

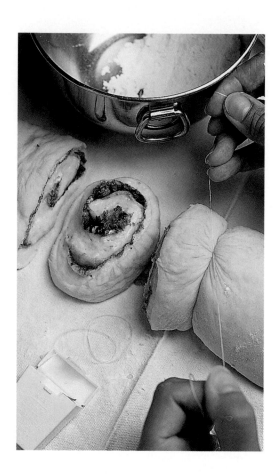

Old-Fashioned Cinnamon Rolls

This comfort food has only 17% of its 165 calories from fat. Surprise your family with these rolls on Christmas morning, and keep the calorie count your secret.

⅓ cup skim milk
⅓ cup reduced-calorie margarine
¼ cup firmly packed brown sugar
1 teaspoon salt
1 package active dry yeast
½ cup warm water (105° to 115°)
½ cup egg substitute
3½ cups bread flour, divided
¾ cup quick-cooking oats, uncooked
   Vegetable cooking spray
¼ cup reduced-calorie margarine, softened
¾ cup firmly packed brown sugar
¼ cup raisins
2 teaspoons ground cinnamon
1 cup sifted powdered sugar
2 tablespoons water

Old-Fashioned Cinnamon Rolls

Combine first 4 ingredients in a saucepan; cook over low heat until margarine melts, stirring occasionally. Let cool to 105° to 115°.

Combine yeast and warm water in a 1-cup liquid measuring cup; let stand 5 minutes.

Combine yeast mixture, milk mixture, egg substitute, 1 cup flour, and oats in a large mixing bowl; beat at medium speed of an electric mixer until blended. Gradually stir in enough remaining flour to make a soft dough.

Turn dough out onto a lightly floured surface, and knead until smooth and elastic (about 8 minutes). Place in a large bowl coated with cooking spray, turning to coat top of dough.

Cover and let rise in a warm place (85°), free from drafts, 1 hour or until doubled in bulk. Punch dough down; cover and let rest 10 minutes.

Divide dough in half; roll each portion into a 12-inch square. Spread each square with 2 tablespoons margarine.

Combine ¾ cup brown sugar, raisins, and cinnamon; sprinkle evenly over each square. Roll dough, jellyroll fashion; pinch seam to seal.

Cut each roll into 1-inch slices. Place rolls, cut side down, in 2 (8-inch) square pans coated with cooking spray. Cover and let rise in a warm place, free from drafts, about 30 minutes or until almost doubled in bulk.

Bake at 375° for 15 to 20 minutes or until golden.

Combine powdered sugar and 2 tablespoons water; drizzle over warm rolls. **Yield:** 2 dozen.

Easy Stollen

Commercial frozen bread dough makes this showy Christmas bread almost effortless.

- ½ cup raisins
- ½ cup chopped pecans
- 2 tablespoons chopped red candied cherries
- 2 tablespoons chopped green candied cherries
- 1½ teaspoons brandy or orange juice
- 1 (16-ounce) loaf frozen bread dough, thawed
- 1 tablespoon butter or margarine, melted
  Brandy Glaze

Combine first 5 ingredients.

Place bread dough on a lightly floured surface; flatten with a rolling pin to 1-inch thickness. Spoon fruit mixture in center of dough, and knead dough until fruit is evenly distributed.

Roll dough to an oval shape, ½ inch thick. Fold in half lengthwise, and seal edges. Place dough on a well-greased baking sheet; brush with butter. Cover and let rise in a warm place (85°), free from drafts, 40 minutes or until doubled in bulk.

Bake at 350° for 25 to 30 minutes or until loaf sounds hollow when tapped. Let cool 10 minutes on a wire rack; drizzle with Brandy Glaze. **Yield:** 1 loaf.

Brandy Glaze

- 1½ cups sifted powdered sugar
- 2 tablespoons brandy or orange juice
- 2 teaspoons fresh lime juice

Combine all ingredients in a small bowl; stir well. **Yield:** about ¾ cup.

Candy Cane Bread

This recipe defines big baking. It yields three large, luscious loaves. Keep one, and give two as gifts.

1½   cups chopped dried apricots
  2   cups boiling water
  1   (16-ounce) carton sour cream
⅓   cup sugar
¼   cup butter or margarine
1½   teaspoons salt
  2   packages dry yeast
½   cup warm water (105° to 115°)
  2   large eggs, lightly beaten
  6   to 6½ cups all-purpose flour, divided
1½   cups chopped maraschino cherries
¼   cup butter or margarine, melted
  1   cup sifted powdered sugar
  1   tablespoon plus 1 to 2 teaspoons milk
     Garnish: candied cherry halves

Combine apricots and boiling water; cover and let stand 1 hour. Drain apricots, and set aside.

Combine sour cream and next 3 ingredients in a heavy saucepan; stir over low heat until butter melts. Let cool to 105° to 115°.

Dissolve yeast in warm water in a large mixing bowl; let stand 5 minutes. Add sour cream mixture, eggs, and 2 cups flour; beat at low speed of an electric mixer until smooth. Stir in enough remaining flour to make a soft dough.

Turn dough out onto a floured surface, and knead until smooth and elastic (8 to 10 minutes). Place in a greased bowl, turning to grease top. Cover and let rise in a warm place (85°), free from drafts, 1 hour or until doubled in bulk.

Punch dough down; divide into thirds. Roll each portion into a 15- x 6-inch rectangle on a lightly floured surface; transfer to greased baking sheets. Make 2-inch cuts into dough at ½-inch intervals on long sides of rectangles, leaving a 2-inch uncut strip down the center of each.

Combine apricots and maraschino cherries; spread down center of each dough rectangle. Fold and overlap strips diagonally over fruit filling in a braided fashion; gently stretch each dough rectangle to measure 22 inches. Curve one end of each to resemble a cane.

Bake at 375° for 15 minutes or until golden. Brush each cane with melted butter; let cool. Combine powdered sugar and milk; stir until smooth, and drizzle over bread. Garnish, if desired.
Yield: 3 loaves.

Alphabet Breadsticks

Using a hot roll mix is a no-fuss way to introduce your child to "homemade" bread.

- 1 (16-ounce) package hot roll mix
- ½ cup (2 ounces) shredded sharp Cheddar cheese
- 1 cup plus 2 tablespoons hot water (120° to 130°)
- 1 egg white, lightly beaten
- 1 tablespoon vegetable oil
  Vegetable cooking spray
- 1 egg white
- 1 tablespoon water
- 1 tablespoon sesame seeds

Combine hot roll mix, yeast from foil packet, and cheese in a large bowl; stir well. Add hot water, beaten egg white, and oil, stirring until dry ingredients are moistened.

Shape dough into a ball. Turn out onto a lightly floured surface, and knead until smooth (about 5 minutes). Cover; let stand 5 minutes.

Divide dough into 24 equal portions; roll each portion into a 12-inch rope. (Cover remaining dough to prevent from drying out.) Shape each rope into a favorite alphabet letter, and place on baking sheets coated with cooking spray.

Combine 1 egg white and 1 tablespoon water; brush over letters, and sprinkle with sesame seeds.

Bake at 375° for about 15 minutes or until golden. Let cool on wire racks.
Yield: 2 dozen.

Super Dinner Rolls

- 7¼ cups bread flour, divided
- ¾ cup sugar
- 1 teaspoon salt
- 2 packages active dry yeast
- 2 cups milk
- ½ cup butter
- 3 large eggs, lightly beaten

Combine 2 cups flour, sugar, salt, and yeast in a large mixing bowl; stir well. Combine milk and butter in a saucepan; heat until butter melts, stirring occasionally. Cool to 120° to 130°. Gradually add liquid mixture to flour mixture. Beat 2 additional minutes at medium speed. Add eggs and ¾ cup flour, beating 2 minutes at medium speed. Gradually stir in enough of remaining 4½ cups flour to make a soft dough.

Turn dough out onto a lightly floured surface; knead until smooth and elastic (about 8 to 10 minutes). Place dough in a large, well-greased bowl, turning to grease top. Cover and let rise in a warm place (85°), free from drafts, 45 minutes or until doubled in bulk.

Punch dough down; divide in half. Divide each half into 11 equal portions; shape each portion into a ball. Place at least 1 inch apart on large greased baking sheets.

Cover and let rise in warm place, free from drafts, 30 minutes or until doubled in bulk.

Bake at 325° for 18 to 20 minutes or until lightly browned. Remove rolls from baking sheets; let cool on wire racks.
Yield: 22 rolls.

Sour Cream Yeast Rolls

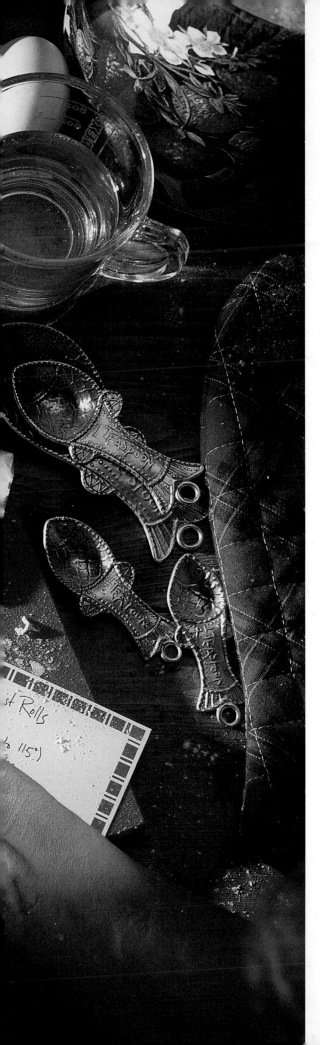

Sour Cream Yeast Rolls

This is a well-loved recipe at Southern Living. *It's an ideal dough to work with because of the velvety texture it gains from sour cream.*

  1 package dry yeast
¼ cup warm water (105° to 115°)
¼ cup butter or margarine
½ cup sour cream
¼ cup sugar
½ teaspoon salt
  1 large egg, lightly beaten
  2 cups all-purpose flour
¼ cup butter or margarine, melted

Combine yeast and warm water in a 1-cup liquid measuring cup; let stand 5 minutes.

Combine ¼ cup butter and next 3 ingredients in a saucepan; heat until butter melts, stirring occasionally. Let cool to 105° to 115°. Transfer to a large bowl; stir in yeast mixture and egg. Gradually add flour, mixing well. Cover and chill at least 8 hours.

Punch dough down; turn out onto a floured surface, and knead 3 or 4 times. Roll dough to ¼-inch thickness, and cut with a 2½-inch biscuit cutter.

Make a crease with the dull edge of a knife just off the center on each round. Brush dough lightly with melted butter. Fold larger side over smaller side so edges will meet; press gently to seal. Repeat procedure with remaining dough. Place 12 rolls each in 2 lightly greased 8-inch round pans.

Cover and let rise in a warm place (85°), free from drafts, 40 minutes or until doubled in bulk. Bake at 375° for 10 to 12 minutes or until golden. **Yield:** 2 dozen.

Variation: To make Cloverleaf Rolls, lightly grease two muffin pans. Shape dough into 1-inch balls; place 3 dough balls in each muffin cup. Cover and let rise in a warm place (85°) free from drafts, 40 minutes or until doubled in bulk. Bake as directed. Brush rolls with melted butter. **Yield:** 2 dozen.

Crispy Prosciutto Pinwheels, page 123

Baked Gouda in Pastry, page 122

Santa's Favorite Snacks

You won't want to leave these nibbles for Santa only. Try some high-flavor dips and spreads or any of four versions of the famed cheese straw. Or sample several puff pastry delicacies, from pinwheels to puffs. They're filled with lots of spice, hot smoked sausage, cheese, or ham. And then slice into two unique cheesecakes—their savory rather than sweet flavors will surprise and satisfy a crowd.

Bacon and Cheese Cracker Stacks

Bacon and Cheese Cracker Stacks

Orange marmalade is a sweet surprise in this crispy cracker snack.

1 (8-ounce) package cream cheese with chives and onion
½ cup (2 ounces) finely shredded Cheddar cheese
¼ cup finely chopped natural almonds, toasted
3 tablespoons orange marmalade
24 slices bacon
48 rectangular buttery crackers

Combine first 4 ingredients in a small bowl; stir well. Cover and chill.

Cook bacon in batches in a large skillet over medium heat 2 to 3 minutes on each side or until lightly browned; drain well on paper towels. Spread 1 tablespoon cheese mixture on 24 crackers. Top each with another cracker. Wrap a slice of bacon around each cracker stack, overlapping bacon ends on bottom. Place, seam side down, on ungreased baking sheets.

Bake at 350° for 15 minutes or until bacon is crisp. Serve immediately. **Yield:** 2 dozen.

Taco Snackers

1 (6-ounce) package Cheddar fish-shape crackers
1 (6-ounce) package plain fish-shape crackers
3 cups crispy wheat cereal squares
2 cups scoop-size corn chips
¼ cup butter or margarine, melted
2 tablespoons dry taco seasoning mix

Combine first 4 ingredients in a large bowl. Combine butter and seasoning mix. Drizzle over cracker mixture, tossing gently to coat. Spread in an ungreased 15- x 10- x 1-inch jellyroll pan.

Bake at 325° for 15 to 20 minutes, stirring every 10 minutes. Remove from oven; let cool. Store in an airtight container. **Yield:** 11 cups.

Easy-as-Pie Cheese Straws

1 (11-ounce) package pie crust mix
1 (5-ounce) jar sharp process cheese spread
¼ teaspoon ground red pepper

Position knife blade in food processor bowl; add all ingredients, and process 30 seconds or until mixture forms a ball, stopping often to scrape down sides.

Use a cookie press fitted with a bar-shaped disk to shape dough into 2½-inch straws, following manufacturer's instructions. Or divide dough in half, and shape each portion into a 7-inch log; wrap in plastic wrap, and chill 1 hour. Cut into ¼-inch slices. Place straws or slices on lightly greased baking sheets.

Bake at 375° for 8 minutes or until lightly browned. Transfer to wire racks to cool. **Yield:** 5 dozen.

Chili-Cheese Straws

2 cups (8 ounces) shredded Monterey Jack cheese with peppers
½ cup butter or margarine, softened
1 cup all-purpose flour
⅓ cup yellow cornmeal
1 teaspoon chili powder
½ teaspoon salt
½ teaspoon ground cumin

Combine cheese and butter, stirring until blended. Gradually add flour and remaining ingredients, stirring until mixture is no longer crumbly and will shape into a ball.

Use a cookie press fitted with a star-shaped disk to shape dough into straws, following manufacturer's instructions. Or divide dough into fourths, and roll each portion into a ¼-inch-thick rectangle on wax paper. Cut into 2- x ½-inch strips with a knife or pastry wheel. Place straws or strips on ungreased baking sheets.

Bake at 375° for 8 minutes or until lightly browned. Transfer to wire racks to cool. **Yield:** about 8 dozen.

Parmesan Cheese Straws

⅔ cup grated Parmesan cheese
½ cup butter or margarine, softened
1 cup all-purpose flour
¼ teaspoon salt
¼ teaspoon ground red pepper
¼ cup milk
　 Pecan halves (optional)

Position knife blade in food processor bowl; add cheese and butter. Process until blended.

Add flour, salt, and pepper to cheese mixture; process about 30 seconds or until mixture forms a ball, stopping often to scrape down sides.

Divide dough in half; roll each portion into a ⅛-inch-thick rectangle, and cut into 2- x ½-inch strips. Or shape dough into ¾-inch balls; flatten each ball to about ⅛-inch thickness.

Place strips or rounds of dough on ungreased baking sheets; brush dough with milk. Top with pecan halves, if desired.

Bake strips at 350° for 7 minutes and rounds for 10 minutes or until lightly browned. Transfer to wire racks to cool. **Yield**: 5 dozen cheese straws or 3 dozen wafers.

Brie Cheese Wafers

½ pound Brie, softened
½ cup butter, softened
2 cups all-purpose flour
¼ teaspoon salt
¼ teaspoon ground red pepper
¼ teaspoon Worcestershire sauce

Position knife blade in food processor bowl; add Brie (with rind) and butter. Process until blended, stopping often to scrape down sides. Add flour and remaining ingredients, pulsing until a soft dough forms.

Divide dough in half, and shape each portion into an 8-inch log; wrap in plastic wrap, and chill 8 hours. Cut into ¼-inch slices. Or use a cookie press fitted with a star-shaped disk to shape dough into straws, following manufacturer's instructions. Place slices or straws on ungreased baking sheets.

Bake at 375° for 8 minutes or until lightly browned. Transfer to wire racks to cool. **Yield:** 5 dozen wafers or 7 dozen cheese straws.

Cheese Straw Showcase

- *Try one of these 4 variations on America's favorite wafer. They range from easy to elegant, and each one sports a different cheese.*

- *If you don't own a cookie press, don't worry. We give you easy options for shaping the dough into logs or rectangles to cut by hand.*

Antipasto Spread with Toast Rounds

Choosing Crackers

Here are our test kitchen staff's top cracker choices for the dips and spreads on these pages:

- *For **Antipasto Spread,** try garlic-flavored Melba toast. It's a sturdy, crisp mild-flavored cracker.*

- *For **Hearts of Palm Spread,** pick Lavash. It's a mild cracker for a salty spread.*

- *For **Marinated Artichoke Dip,** choose Wheatberry crackers. They're slightly sweet to complement a tangy dip.*

- *For **Hot Spinach-Jalapeño Dip,** get big scoop corn chips or stone-ground thin wheat crackers. They're sturdy dippers for a creamy, soft dip.*

Antipasto Spread with Toast Rounds

1 (13-ounce) package French baguettes
⅓ cup olive oil
1 (14-ounce) can artichoke hearts, drained and finely chopped
1 (4-ounce) can sliced mushrooms, drained and finely chopped
1 (2-ounce) jar diced pimiento, drained
¾ cup pitted ripe olives, chopped
¼ cup chopped green pepper
¼ cup chopped celery
¾ cup olive oil
¼ cup white wine vinegar
2 tablespoons water
1 tablespoon dried Italian seasoning
¼ teaspoon pepper
⅛ teaspoon salt
1 clove garlic, crushed

Cut bread with a serrated knife into ⅜-inch thick rounds. Lightly brush tops with ⅓ cup olive oil; place on baking sheets. Bake at 400° for 8 to 10 minutes or until crisp. Set aside.

Combine artichokes and next 5 ingredients. Combine ¾ cup oil and remaining 6 ingredients in a jar; cover tightly, and shake vigorously. Pour over artichoke mixture; cover and chill up to 1 week. Drain before serving; serve with toast rounds. **Yield:** 4 dozen appetizer servings.

Hearts of Palm Spread

1 (14-ounce) can hearts of palm, drained and chopped
1 cup (4 ounces) shredded mozzarella cheese
¾ cup mayonnaise or salad dressing
½ cup grated Parmesan cheese
¼ cup sour cream
2 tablespoons minced green onions

Combine all ingredients; spoon into a greased 9-inch quiche dish.

Bake at 350° for 20 minutes or until bubbly. Serve hot with crackers. **Yield:** about 2 cups.

Marinated Artichoke Dip

2 (6-ounce) jars marinated artichoke hearts
1 (11-ounce) log goat cheese
½ (8-ounce) package cream cheese, softened
¾ cup mayonnaise
½ cup grated Parmesan cheese, divided
½ cup chopped pecans, toasted
2 green onions, chopped
1½ tablespoons all-purpose flour
2 teaspoons dried Italian seasoning
¾ cup soft whole wheat breadcrumbs
1 tablespoon butter or margarine, melted

Drain artichoke hearts well; chop. Combine goat cheese, cream cheese, mayonnaise, and ¼ cup Parmesan cheese in a mixing bowl; beat at low speed of an electric mixer until smooth. Stir in artichokes, pecans, and next 3 ingredients. Spoon into an ungreased shallow 1½-quart casserole.

Combine remaining ¼ cup Parmesan cheese, breadcrumbs, and butter; toss gently. Sprinkle over dip.

Bake, uncovered, at 350° for 20 minutes or until thoroughly heated and topping is browned. Serve hot with bagel chips. **Yield:** 4½ cups.

Hot Spinach-Jalapeño Dip

2 (10-ounce) packages frozen chopped spinach
¼ cup butter or margarine
2 tablespoons all-purpose flour
½ cup evaporated milk
1 (6-ounce) roll jalapeño cheese, cubed
2 tablespoons finely chopped onion
1 teaspoon Worcestershire sauce
¾ teaspoon celery salt
¾ teaspoon garlic powder
½ teaspoon ground black pepper
¼ teaspoon lemon juice
Dash of ground red pepper
Dash of hot sauce
½ cup soft, buttered breadcrumbs

Cook spinach according to package directions, omitting salt. Drain, reserving ½ cup liquid. Melt butter in a saucepan over low heat; add flour, stirring until smooth. Cook, stirring constantly, 1 minute.

Add spinach, reserved ½ cup liquid, milk, and remaining ingredients except breadcrumbs; stir until smooth. Spoon into a greased 1-quart casserole; sprinkle with breadcrumbs.

Bake at 350° for 25 minutes. Serve hot with crackers. **Yield:** 4 cups.

Creamed Shrimp in Mini Pastry Shells

2 (9½-ounce) packages frozen mini puff pastry shells
1½ pounds unpeeled, medium-size fresh shrimp
⅔ cup dry white wine
½ cup chopped onion
2 tablespoons chopped fresh parsley
½ teaspoon salt
3 tablespoons butter or margarine
3 tablespoons all-purpose flour
1 cup milk
1 cup (4 ounces) shredded Swiss cheese
2 teaspoons lemon juice
½ teaspoon pepper

Bake pastry shells according to package directions; let cool. Set aside.

Peel and devein shrimp, if desired.

Combine wine and next 3 ingredients in a saucepan; bring to a boil. Add shrimp, and cook 3 to 5 minutes. Drain, reserving ¼ cup liquid. Chop shrimp, and set aside.

Melt butter in a large saucepan over low heat; add flour, stirring until smooth. Cook 1 minute, stirring constantly. Gradually add milk, and cook over medium heat, stirring constantly, until mixture is thickened and bubbly.

Add cheese, stirring until cheese melts. Gradually stir in shrimp, reserved ¼ cup liquid, lemon juice, and pepper.

Spoon mixture into a greased 2-quart shallow baking dish. (Cover baking dish, and chill up to 8 hours at this point if you wish. Before serving, let dish stand at room temperature 30 minutes.)

Bake, covered, at 350° for 30 minutes or until thoroughly heated. Spoon mixture into baked pastry shells, and serve immediately. **Yield:** 25 appetizer servings.

Pastry Plan B

• *You can substitute 4 (9-inch) refrigerated piecrusts for puff pastry shells (recipe at left). Cut 12 (2½-inch) circles from each piecrust, and fit circles into miniature (1¾-inch) muffin pans; prick pastry with a fork. Bake at 450° for 8 to 10 minutes.*

Crabmeat-Stuffed Oysters

You can substitute 2 (12-ounce) containers fresh oysters. Bake according to recipe directions in shell-shaped baking dishes found in kitchen shops.

    2   dozen fresh oysters in the shell
    1   pound lump crabmeat, drained
    ½   cup soft breadcrumbs
    ⅓   cup milk
    ¼   cup mayonnaise
    2   teaspoons dried onion flakes
    2   teaspoons chopped fresh parsley
    ½   teaspoon baking powder
    ¼   teaspoon garlic salt
    ¼   teaspoon ground white pepper
    1   large egg, lightly beaten
    2   tablespoons thinly sliced green
        onions
    1   (2-ounce) jar sliced pimiento,
        drained

Scrub oyster shells, and open, discarding tops. Loosen oysters from shell bottoms; arrange shells, with oysters, in a 15- x 10- x 1-inch jellyroll pan. Set aside.

Combine crabmeat and next 9 ingredients. Spoon mixture evenly over oysters; sprinkle with onions. Place 1 or 2 pimiento strips on each oyster. (Reserve remaining pimiento for another use.)

Bake at 400° for 15 minutes or until thoroughly heated. **Yield:** 6 appetizer servings.

Angel Wings

Kids will love these. Napkins are a necessity.

    18 chicken wings (about 5 pounds)
    ½   cup sugar
    ½   cup water
    ½   cup soy sauce
    ¼   cup orange juice
    2   tablespoons vegetable oil
    1   teaspoon grated fresh ginger
    ½   teaspoon garlic powder

Remove and discard wing tips; cut wings in half at joint. Place wing pieces in a 13- x 9- x 2-inch baking dish.

Combine sugar and remaining 6 ingredients; pour mixture over chicken, turning to coat. Cover and chill 8 hours.

Remove chicken from marinade, reserving marinade.

Place chicken on a lightly greased 15- x 10- x 1-inch jellyroll pan.

Bring marinade to a boil in a small saucepan; reduce heat, and simmer 5 minutes.

Bake chicken at 350° for 40 minutes or until done, basting twice with marinade. Place chicken on a serving platter; serve warm. **Yield:** 3 dozen.

Pork Tenderloin with Mustard Sauce

It's okay for pork to have a slightly pink color when it's cooked. As long as the temperature reaches 160°, the pork is done.

    ½   cup teriyaki sauce
    2   tablespoons brown sugar
    ¼   cup bourbon
    4   (¾-pound) pork tenderloins
        Mustard Sauce
        Commercial party rolls

Combine first 3 ingredients in a shallow baking dish or a large heavy-duty, zip-top plastic bag. Add tenderloins; cover or seal, and chill 8 hours, turning meat occasionally.

Remove from marinade, discarding marinade. Place on a rack in a shallow roasting pan.

Bake at 400° for 30 minutes or until a meat thermometer inserted into thickest portion registers 160°. Thinly slice, and serve with Mustard Sauce on party rolls. Yield: 25 appetizer servings.

Mustard Sauce

- ⅔ cup sour cream
- ⅔ cup mayonnaise
- 2 tablespoons dry mustard
- 3 to 4 green onions, finely chopped

Combine all ingredients; cover and chill. Yield: 1⅓ cups.

Pork Tenderloin with Mustard Sauce

Sausage-Date Balls

- 1 pound ground pork sausage
- 2 cups biscuit mix
- ½ cup finely chopped pecans
- 1 (8-ounce) package pitted dates, chopped

Combine all ingredients; stir well, and shape into 1-inch balls. Place on lightly greased baking sheets.

Bake at 350° for 20 minutes or until browned. Serve warm or at room temperature. Yield: 4½ dozen.

Taco Tassies

- 1 pound ground round
- 2 tablespoons dry taco seasoning mix
- 2 tablespoons water
- ½ cup sour cream
- 1 tablespoon taco sauce
- ⅓ cup coarsely crushed tortilla chips
- ¾ cup (3 ounces) shredded Monterey Jack cheese with peppers
  Tortilla chips
  Additional taco sauce
  Garnishes: sour cream, fresh cilantro

Combine first 3 ingredients. Divide into 24 equal portions. Using a fork, press each portion into a miniature (1¾-inch) muffin pan cup to form a shell.

Combine sour cream, taco sauce, and crushed tortilla chips; spoon 1 teaspoon mixture into each shell.

Bake at 425° for 10 minutes. Sprinkle with cheese, and bake 5 additional minutes. Remove from pans, and serve immediately on a layer of tortilla chips with additional taco sauce. Garnish, if desired. Yield: 2 dozen.

Freeze Ahead

- *You can freeze Sausage-Date Balls after cooking. Chill thoroughly; then freeze in an airtight container. Thaw at room temperature.*

Crunchy Potato Bites

1 cup cooked mashed potatoes
1 cup ground cooked ham
½ cup (2 ounces) shredded Swiss cheese
2 tablespoons chopped green onions
3 tablespoons mayonnaise
1 teaspoon prepared mustard
¼ teaspoon hot sauce
Dash of pepper
1 large egg, lightly beaten
1 cup crushed corn flakes

Combine all ingredients except corn flakes. Shape mixture into 1-inch balls; coat with crushed corn flakes. Place on lightly greased baking sheets.

Bake at 350° for 30 minutes. Serve warm. **Yield:** 2 dozen.

Spinach Pom-Poms

You can freeze unbaked Spinach Pom-Poms on a jellyroll pan up to one week. To serve, let stand at room temperature one hour; bake as directed.

2 (10-ounce) packages frozen chopped spinach, thawed and drained
2 cups herb-seasoned stuffing mix, crushed
1 cup grated Parmesan cheese
⅓ cup butter or margarine, softened
Dash of ground nutmeg
6 large eggs, lightly beaten
Spicy mustard

Squeeze spinach between paper towels until barely moist. Combine spinach, stuffing mix, and next 4 ingredients; shape into 2-inch balls. Place balls on a lightly greased 15- x 10- x 1-inch jelly-roll pan; cover and chill 8 hours.

Bake at 350° for 15 to 20 minutes or until hot. Drain on paper towels. Serve with your favorite spicy mustard. **Yield:** 14 servings.

Baked Horseradish Squares

You can freeze these morsels, unbaked, up to one week. To serve, let stand 10 minutes. Remove crusts, quarter slices, and bake as directed.

½ pound cooked ham, coarsely chopped
1 small onion, quartered
8 ounces extra-sharp Cheddar cheese, coarsely chopped
1½ tablespoons prepared horseradish
½ teaspoon salt
½ teaspoon hot pepper sauce
¼ teaspoon pepper
1 (16-ounce) loaf very thinly sliced sandwich bread
Paprika

Position knife blade in food processor bowl; add ham and onion. Process until finely chopped. Remove from bowl; set aside. Add Cheddar cheese to processor bowl; process until finely chopped. Return ham and onion to processor bowl. Add horseradish and next 3 ingredients; process just until mixture begins to form a ball.

Spread about 1 tablespoon mixture on each bread slice. Place slices on ungreased baking sheets; cover and freeze about 20 minutes or until spread is firm. Remove crusts; cut each slice into 4 squares. Sprinkle with paprika.

Bake at 400° for 12 to 14 minutes. Remove from oven; serve immediately. **Yield:** 9 dozen.

Broccoli Bites

1 small onion, chopped
1 clove garlic, minced
2 tablespoons vegetable oil
1 (10-ounce) package frozen
chopped broccoli, thawed
6 large eggs, lightly beaten
2½ cups (10 ounces) shredded Gouda
cheese
⅓ cup Italian-seasoned breadcrumbs
¾ teaspoon dried oregano
½ teaspoon pepper
1 (2-ounce) jar diced pimiento,
drained
¼ cup sesame seeds
⅓ cup grated Parmesan cheese

Cook onion and garlic in hot oil in a
large skillet over medium-high heat, stirring constantly, until tender. Add broccoli; cook just until crisp-tender. Remove
from heat.

Combine eggs and next 5 ingredients
in a large bowl, stirring well. Stir in
broccoli mixture. Spoon into a lightly
greased 13- x 9- x 2-inch baking dish.

Toast sesame seeds in a small nonstick skillet over high heat, stirring constantly, 2 minutes or until golden.
Sprinkle sesame seeds and Parmesan
cheese over broccoli mixture.

Bake, uncovered, at 350° for 20 to 25
minutes or until browned. Let stand
15 minutes. Cut into small squares, and
serve warm. **Yield:** 3 dozen.

Ham-Pineapple Nibbles

*Commercial crescent rolls encase this
savory ham and pineapple filling.*

1 large egg, lightly beaten
1½ cups ground cooked ham
½ cup (2 ounces) shredded
mozzarella cheese
¼ cup soft breadcrumbs
¼ teaspoon rubbed sage
2 green onions, sliced
1 (8¼-ounce) can crushed
pineapple, drained
3 (8-ounce) cans refrigerated
crescent rolls

Combine first 7 ingredients in a large
bowl; set aside.

Separate each package of rolls into 4
rectangles, pressing perforations to seal.
Roll each rectangle into an 8- x 4-inch
rectangle; cut each crosswise into thirds.

Place about 1 tablespoon ham mixture in center of each third of dough.
Fold dough over ham mixture, pressing
edges to seal; crimp with a fork. Place on
ungreased baking sheets.

Bake at 375° for 10 minutes or until
golden. **Yield:** 3 dozen.

Italian Biscuit Flatbread

This quick bread, which relies on convenience products, teams perfectly with salads and soups. After serving it to friends, be prepared to share the recipe.

- ⅔ cup freshly grated Parmesan cheese
- ½ cup mayonnaise
- ½ teaspoon garlic powder
- ½ teaspoon dried oregano
- 3 green onions, finely chopped
- 1 (10-ounce) can refrigerated buttermilk biscuits

Combine first 5 ingredients, and set aside.

Roll each biscuit to a 5-inch circle on a lightly floured surface; place on baking sheets.

Spread cheese mixture evenly over biscuits, leaving a ¼-inch border.

Bake at 400° for 10 to 11 minutes or until golden. Serve immediately with soup or salad, or cut into wedges to serve as an appetizer. **Yield:** 10 servings.

Note: You can assemble and chill this flatbread up to 3 hours before baking.

Provençal Pizza Bites

- 1 (10-ounce) can refrigerated pizza dough
- 1½ cups firmly packed fresh basil leaves
- ¾ cup freshly grated Parmesan cheese, divided
- ⅔ cup chopped walnuts, toasted and divided
- 2 cloves garlic, cut in half
- ⅓ cup olive oil
- 1½ cups (6 ounces) shredded mozzarella cheese
- ½ pound smoked turkey, cubed
- 1 cup diced sweet red pepper
- 1 (6-ounce) jar marinated artichoke hearts, drained and chopped

Unroll pizza dough, and press into bottom of a greased 13- x 9- x 2-inch pan. Set aside.

Position knife blade in food processor bowl; add basil, ½ cup Parmesan cheese, ⅓ cup toasted walnuts, and garlic. Process 1 minute or until smooth, stopping once to scrape down sides. With processor running, pour olive oil through food chute in a slow, steady stream until combined.

Spread basil mixture over pizza dough, leaving a ½-inch border on all sides. Sprinkle with mozzarella cheese, turkey, red pepper, artichokes, remaining ¼ cup Parmesan, and remaining ⅓ cup walnuts.

Bake, uncovered, at 425° for 30 minutes or until crust is golden and mozzarella cheese melts. Cut into rectangles. **Yield:** 18 appetizer servings.

New Orleans Style Canapés

Olive salad is a component of the New Orleans Muffuletta sandwich. Here we repackage the colorful chopped salad as a filling for these flaky mouthfuls.

1 (12-ounce) jar pickled mixed vegetables, drained
¼ cup pimiento-stuffed olive slices, chopped
2 ounces thinly sliced salami, finely chopped
1 tablespoon minced garlic
1 tablespoon olive oil
2 (10-ounce) cans refrigerated flaky biscuits
½ cup finely shredded provolone cheese

Chop mixed vegetables. Combine vegetables, olives, and next 3 ingredients. Cover and chill at least 1 hour.

Bake biscuits according to package directions. Let cool slightly. Using a melon baller or small spoon, carefully scoop out center of 16 biscuits. (Reserve remaining biscuits for another use.)

Stir cheese into olive salad mixture. Spoon 1 heaping tablespoon into each hollowed-out biscuit.

Bake at 400° for 8 to 10 minutes or until cheese melts. Serve warm. **Yield:** 16 appetizers.

Provençal Pizza Bite

New Orleans Style Canapés

Baked Gouda in Pastry

You can assemble this appetizer in advance; just cover and chill it up to 24 hours before baking.

- ½ **(17¼-ounce) package frozen puff pastry sheets**
- 1 **cup finely chopped pecans, divided**
- 2 **(7-ounce) rounds Gouda cheese, rinds removed**

Thaw 1 pastry sheet according to package directions; reserve second sheet in freezer for another use. Cut thawed pastry sheet in half, and roll each half on a lightly floured surface to a 9-inch square.

Sprinkle ¼ cup pecans in center of each pastry square. Place cheese rounds

Baked Gouda in Pastry

over pecans; sprinkle ¼ cup pecans over each cheese round. Bring corners of each pastry square to center of each cheese round. Fold pastry to fit cheese round; twist top to completely enclose cheese. Place pastries on a lightly greased baking sheet.

Bake at 400° for 25 minutes or until puffed and golden. Transfer to serving plates, and serve immediately. **Yield:** 12 appetizer servings.

Cajun Hot Puffs

Unbaked Cajun Hot Puffs can be frozen up to three months. Let thaw, and bake according to directions.

  1 **(17¼-ounce) package frozen puff pastry, thawed**
     Cornmeal
  ½ **pound hot smoked link sausage**
  1 **(4½-ounce) can sliced pickled jalapeño peppers, drained**

Roll 1 pastry sheet into a 15- x 12-inch rectangle on a surface lightly sprinkled with cornmeal. Cut into 3-inch squares.

Cut sausage into ¼-inch slices. Cut each slice in half crosswise. Place 1 sausage slice and 1 jalapeño slice in center of each pastry square. Fold corners to center, slightly overlapping edges.

Place filled pastries, seam side down, on greased baking sheets sprinkled with cornmeal. Repeat procedure with remaining pastry, sausage, and jalapeño peppers.

Bake at 400° for 12 to 15 minutes. Serve immediately. **Yield:** 40 appetizers.

Crispy Prosciutto Pinwheels

  1 **(17¼-ounce) package frozen puff pastry, thawed**
  1 **(4.25-ounce) jar champagne mustard**
  1 **cup grated Parmesan cheese**
 1½ **tablespoons dried oregano**
  2 **teaspoons garlic powder**
  8 **ounces thinly sliced prosciutto**
  1 **large egg, lightly beaten**

Place 1 pastry sheet on a work surface; spread half of mustard evenly over pastry. Combine cheese, oregano, and garlic powder; sprinkle half of cheese mixture over mustard. Arrange half of prosciutto slices evenly over cheese mixture. Lightly press prosciutto into cheese.

Roll up pastry, jellyroll fashion, until both rolls meet in the middle. Repeat procedure with remaining pastry sheet, mustard, cheese mixture, and prosciutto. Cover and chill rolls at least 30 minutes.

Cut rolls crosswise into ½-inch slices. (Slices will resemble a figure 8.) Place slices on lightly greased baking sheets. Brush tops with egg.

Bake at 350° for 25 minutes or until puffed and golden. Serve warm or at room temperature. **Yield:** about 3½ dozen.

The Fluff about Puff Pastry

These snack recipes present puff pastry in three very different shapes. Here are some hints when you're ready to try a puff pastry recipe.

- *Two sheets come in each 17¼-ounce package.*

- *Read the pastry package for thawing instructions. It's important to thaw the pastry sheets properly before unfolding them, or they may crumble.*

- *Bake or chill a puff pastry recipe immediately after preparing it, or the pastry may fail to puff in the oven.*

Crispy Prosciutto Pinwheels

Chicken Nacho Cheesecake

Crab and Muenster Cheesecake

Chicken Nacho Cheesecake

1⅔ cups finely crushed tortilla chips
¼ cup butter or margarine, melted
3 (8-ounce) packages cream cheese, softened
4 large eggs
½ cup mayonnaise
1 (1.25-ounce) package taco seasoning mix
2 tablespoons all-purpose flour
1½ cups drained and finely chopped canned premium chunk white chicken
1½ cups (6 ounces) shredded colby-Monterey Jack cheese blend
1 (8-ounce) carton sour cream
    Toppings: sliced ripe olives, cooked whole kernel corn, chopped green onions, chopped fresh tomato
    Picante sauce or salsa

Combine tortilla chips and butter; stir well. Firmly press into bottom of a 10-inch springform pan; set aside.

Beat cream cheese at high speed of an electric mixer until creamy. Add eggs, one at a time, beating well after each addition. Add mayonnaise, taco seasoning mix, and flour; beat at low speed until smooth. Stir in chicken and cheese. Pour batter into prepared pan.

Bake at 325° for 55 minutes. Spread sour cream on top of cheesecake; bake 10 additional minutes. Let cool to room temperature in pan on a wire rack; cover and chill at least 8 hours.

To serve, carefully remove sides of pan. Arrange toppings on cheesecake. Serve with picante sauce. **Yield:** one 10-inch cheesecake.

Crab and Muenster Cheesecake

This cheesecake is great for a busy host—it can be frozen up to two weeks. To freeze, bake as directed, and let cool completely on a wire rack. Remove sides of pan, cover the cheesecake tightly, and freeze. Thaw in refrigerator.

1¼ cups fine, dry breadcrumbs
3 tablespoons butter or margarine, melted
2 (8-ounce) packages cream cheese, softened
3 large eggs
⅔ cup mayonnaise
2 tablespoons all-purpose flour
12 ounces fresh crabmeat, drained and flaked
1¼ cups (5 ounces) shredded Muenster cheese
¼ cup minced fresh chives
1 (2-ounce) jar diced pimiento, drained
    Garnish: fresh chives

Combine breadcrumbs and butter; stir well. Firmly press crumb mixture into bottom of a 9-inch springform pan; set aside.

Beat cream cheese at high speed of an electric mixer until creamy. Add eggs, one at a time, beating well after each addition. Add mayonnaise and flour; mix until blended. Stir in crabmeat and next 3 ingredients. Pour into prepared pan.

Bake at 325° for 1 hour or until center is set. Let cool to room temperature in pan on a wire rack; cover and chill at least 8 hours.

To serve, carefully remove sides of pan. Garnish, if desired. **Yield:** one 9-inch cheesecake.

Mediterranean Ravioli, page 137

Crowd Pleasing Casseroles

Feast on one of fifteen family favorite casseroles. Our assortment offers seafood, chicken, turkey, pork, and beef, and all can be made ahead. Each is smothered in a rich red sauce, cream sauce, or lots of cheese. And two vegetarian favorites, Garden Lasagna and Mediterranean Ravioli, round out the chapter, providing ultimate holiday comfort food.

Enchiladas with Red Sauce

This recipe is packed with earthy flavors of the Old West.

- 1 pound ground beef
- 1 large onion, chopped
- 1 tablespoon plus 2 teaspoons all-purpose flour
- 1 tablespoon chili powder
- 2 teaspoons garlic powder
- 1 teaspoon salt
- ½ teaspoon ground cumin
- ¼ teaspoon rubbed sage
- 1 (14.5-ounce) can stewed tomatoes, undrained
  Red Sauce
- 12 (6-inch) corn tortillas
- 1 cup finely chopped onion
- 1 cup sliced ripe olives
- 1 (8-ounce) package shredded colby-Monterey Jack cheese blend
  Sour cream
  Additional sliced ripe olives

Brown ground beef and onion in a large skillet, stirring until meat crumbles. Drain and return mixture to skillet. Add flour and next 5 ingredients, stirring well. Add tomatoes with liquid; stir well. Bring to a boil; cover, reduce heat, and simmer 10 to 15 minutes, stirring occasionally. Pour 1½ cups Red Sauce into a 13- x 9- x 2-inch baking dish. Set aside.

Wrap tortillas in aluminum foil, and heat at 350° for 12 to 15 minutes or until softened. Combine 1 cup chopped onion and 1 cup olives; stir well. Work with 1 tortilla at a time, keeping remaining tortillas covered and warm. Sprinkle 2 heaping tablespoonfuls olive mixture down center of tortilla. Top with ¼ cup meat mixture. Roll tortilla tightly, and place in prepared dish, seam side down. Repeat with remaining tortillas. Pour remaining Red Sauce over tortillas.

Cover and bake at 350° for 15 minutes or until thoroughly heated. Uncover and sprinkle with cheese.

Bake, uncovered, 5 additional minutes or until cheese melts. Top enchiladas with sour cream and additional olives. **Yield:** 6 servings.

Red Sauce

- 8 cloves garlic, crushed
- ½ cup butter or margarine, melted
- ½ cup all-purpose flour
- 2 (8-ounce) cans tomato sauce
- 2 cups canned diluted beef broth
- 2 tablespoons chili powder
- 2 teaspoons rubbed sage
- 2 teaspoons ground cumin

Cook garlic in butter in a large saucepan over medium heat, stirring constantly, 1 to 2 minutes. Gradually stir in flour. Cook, stirring constantly, 1 minute. Gradually add tomato sauce and broth; add remaining ingredients. Cook, stirring constantly, until smooth and thickened. **Yield:** 4 cups.

Enchiladas with Red Sauce

Lasagna in a Bun

Serve this hearty Italian version of a sloppy joe with a salad and light vinaigrette for a heart-healthy meal.

6 (3-ounce) French-style rolls
½ pound ground round
½ cup finely chopped onion
1 teaspoon dried Italian seasoning
½ teaspoon salt
1 (8-ounce) can no-salt-added tomato sauce
1 egg white
¾ cup (3 ounces) shredded part-skim mozzarella cheese, divided
⅓ cup part-skim ricotta cheese
3 tablespoons grated Parmesan cheese
½ teaspoon dried Italian seasoning

Cut a thin slice from top of each roll. Hollow out rolls, leaving ½-inch-thick shells; set aside. (Reserve breadcrumbs for another use.)

Brown ground round in a nonstick skillet over medium heat, stirring until it crumbles. Drain and pat dry with paper towels. Wipe drippings from skillet with a paper towel. Return beef to skillet.

Add onion and next 3 ingredients; cover and cook over low heat 5 minutes. Uncover; cook 5 minutes, stirring often.

Combine egg white, half of mozzarella, ricotta, Parmesan, and Italian seasoning. Spoon ¼ cup meat mixture into each roll; top with 2 tablespoons cheese mixture, and sprinkle evenly with remaining mozzarella. Replace roll tops. Place sandwiches in a large baking dish.

Cover and bake at 400° for 20 to 25 minutes or until thoroughly heated. **Yield:** 6 sandwiches.

Tipsy Chicken and Dressing

In this dish, dressing is teamed with chicken, not turkey. And instead of being stuffed, the bird is layered with other ingredients to make a one-dish meal.

1 (8-ounce) package cornbread stuffing mix
3 slices bread, crumbled
2 large eggs, lightly beaten
1 (14½-ounce) can chicken broth, undiluted
1 small onion, finely chopped
1 stalk celery, finely chopped
1 (14-ounce) can artichoke hearts, drained and quartered
8 skinned and boned chicken breast halves
8 (1-ounce) slices Swiss cheese
1 (10¾-ounce) can cream of celery soup, undiluted
1 cup dry white wine
½ teaspoon dried basil
4 mushrooms, sliced
¼ cup grated Parmesan cheese
2 tablespoons minced fresh parsley
   Garnish: additional fresh parsley sprigs

Combine first 6 ingredients; stir well. Divide mixture among 8 greased individual 2-cup baking dishes. Place 3 artichoke quarters in middle of dressing mixture in each dish; place chicken over artichokes. Top with Swiss cheese.

Combine soup, wine, and basil; pour over chicken. Top with mushrooms, Parmesan cheese, and minced parsley.

Cover and bake at 350° for 40 minutes. Uncover and bake 10 additional minutes. Garnish, if desired. **Yield:** 8 servings.

Freeze Ahead

• *Freeze the Lasagna in a Bun sandwiches before baking, if desired. Wrap tightly in aluminum foil, and freeze up to one month. Thaw and bake, still in foil packages, at 400° for 20 to 25 minutes or until thoroughly heated.*

Chicken-Cheddar Tetrazzini

Chicken-Cheddar Tetrazzini

1 (3- to 4-pound) broiler-fryer
1 teaspoon salt
1 teaspoon pepper
1 (8-ounce) package spaghetti
1 large green pepper, seeded and chopped
1 cup sliced fresh mushrooms
1 small onion, chopped
¼ cup butter or margarine, melted
¼ cup all-purpose flour
½ teaspoon salt
½ teaspoon garlic powder
½ teaspoon poultry seasoning
½ teaspoon pepper
1 cup half-and-half
2 cups (8 ounces) shredded sharp Cheddar cheese, divided
1 (10¾-ounce) can cream of mushroom soup, undiluted
¾ cup grated Parmesan cheese, divided
¼ cup sherry
1 (4-ounce) jar diced pimiento, drained
1 teaspoon paprika
¾ cup sliced almonds, toasted

Place broiler-fryer in a Dutch oven, and cover with water. Add 1 teaspoon salt and 1 teaspoon pepper, and bring to a boil. Cover, reduce heat, and simmer 1 hour or until tender. Remove chicken from broth, reserving broth. Let chicken cool to touch. Bone and shred chicken.

Add enough water to reserved broth to measure 3 quarts. Bring to a boil. Cook spaghetti in broth according to package directions. Drain and set aside.

Cook green pepper, mushrooms, and onion in butter in a Dutch oven over medium heat, stirring constantly, until tender. Add flour and next 4 ingredients; stir until smooth. Cook, stirring constantly, 1 minute. Gradually stir in half-and-half, and cook until thickened. Add ¾ cup Cheddar cheese, stirring until cheese melts. Add shredded chicken, mushroom soup, ½ cup Parmesan cheese, sherry, and pimiento; stir well.

Combine chicken mixture and spaghetti, tossing gently. Spread in a greased 13- x 9- x 2-inch baking dish.

Bake, uncovered, at 350° for 20 to 25 minutes or until thoroughly heated. Combine remaining ¼ cup Parmesan cheese and paprika. Sprinkle remaining 1¼ cups Cheddar cheese in diagonal rows across top of casserole. Repeat procedure with almonds and Parmesan mixture.

Bake 5 additional minutes or until Cheddar melts. **Yield:** 6 to 8 servings.

King Ranch Chicken

This Southwestern casserole is named for the King Ranch in Kingsville, Texas, where it originated.

- 4 skinned and boned chicken breast halves
- ¼ teaspoon salt
- ¼ teaspoon pepper
- 2 tablespoons butter or margarine
- 1 medium-size green pepper, seeded and chopped
- 1 medium onion, chopped
- 2 (10-ounce) cans diced tomatoes with green chiles, undrained
- 1 (10¾-ounce) can cream of mushroom soup, undiluted
- 1 (10¾-ounce) can cream of chicken soup, undiluted
- 12 (6-inch) corn tortillas, cut into quarters
- 2 cups (8 ounces) shredded Cheddar cheese, divided

Sprinkle chicken with salt and pepper; place in a greased baking dish.

Bake at 325° for 20 minutes; let cool. Coarsely chop chicken; set aside.

Melt butter in a large skillet over medium heat; add green pepper and onion, and cook, stirring constantly, until crisp-tender. Remove from heat, and stir in chicken, tomatoes, and soups.

Place 4 tortillas in bottom of lightly greased 13- x 9- x 2-inch baking dish; top with one-third of chicken mixture, and sprinkle with ⅔ cup Cheddar cheese. Repeat layers, reserving last ⅔ cup cheese.

Bake, uncovered, at 325° for 35 minutes; sprinkle with reserved cheese, and bake 5 additional minutes. Let stand 5 minutes before serving. **Yield:** 6 to 8 servings.

Ham and Turkey Spaghetti

A cheesy white sauce dresses this pasta. It's a pleasant diversion from typical tomato-topped spaghetti.

- 1 (8-ounce) package thin spaghetti, uncooked
- 2 tablespoons butter or margarine
- 6 green onions, sliced
- 1½ cups sliced fresh mushrooms
- 1½ cups chopped cooked ham
- 1½ cups chopped cooked turkey or chicken
- 1 (12-ounce) carton nonfat cottage cheese
- 1 (8-ounce) carton reduced-fat sour cream
- 2 tablespoons milk
- ¼ teaspoon salt
- ¼ teaspoon celery salt
- ¼ to ½ teaspoon pepper
- 1 cup (4 ounces) shredded reduced-fat sharp Cheddar cheese

Cook spaghetti according to package directions; drain and set aside.

Melt butter in a skillet over medium-high heat; add green onions and mushrooms, and cook, stirring constantly, until crisp-tender. Add ham and turkey; toss gently. Set aside.

Combine cottage cheese and next 5 ingredients in a large bowl; add pasta and meat mixture. Toss gently. Spoon mixture into a lightly greased 13- x 9- x 2-inch baking dish.

Cover and bake at 350° for 45 minutes. Uncover; sprinkle with shredded cheese. Bake, uncovered, 5 additional minutes. **Yield:** 8 servings.

Shredded Chicken Shortcut

- Boil a broiler-fryer in a Dutch oven in water to cover, or roast it in the oven. Let it cool completely; then bone it, and shred or chop the meat. Cover and store in the refrigerator. You'll be one step ahead when you prepare the chicken casseroles in this chapter.

Turkey-Noodle-Poppyseed Casserole

1 (8-ounce) package medium-size egg noodles, uncooked
½ cup chopped onion
¼ cup chopped green pepper
¼ cup butter or margarine, melted
3 tablespoons all-purpose flour
3 cups milk
¼ cup grated Parmesan cheese
1 tablespoon poppyseeds
1 teaspoon salt
⅛ teaspoon ground red pepper
3 cups diced cooked turkey
1 (4-ounce) jar diced pimiento, drained
2 tablespoons grated Parmesan cheese

Cook noodles according to package directions. Drain well, and set aside.

Cook onion and green pepper in butter in a Dutch oven over medium-high heat, stirring constantly, until tender; add flour, stirring until smooth. Cook, stirring constantly, 1 minute. Gradually add milk; cook over medium heat, stirring constantly, until thickened and bubbly. Stir in noodles, ¼ cup Parmesan cheese, poppyseeds, and next 3 ingredients; add pimiento, and stir gently.

Spoon mixture into a lightly greased 13- x 9- x 2-inch baking dish. (If desired, cover and chill 8 hours. Let stand at room temperature 30 minutes before baking.)

Bake, covered, at 350° for 45 minutes. Uncover; sprinkle with 2 tablespoons Parmesan. Bake, uncovered, 10 additional minutes or until thoroughly heated. **Yield:** 6 to 8 servings.

Note: You can freeze the unbaked casserole. To bake, thaw in refrigerator 24 hours. Remove from refrigerator, and let stand at room temperature 30 minutes. Bake as directed above.

Turkey-Noodle-Poppyseed Casserole

Country Ham 'n' Scrambled Egg Casserole

¼ cup butter or margarine
½ cup all-purpose flour
1 quart milk
¼ teaspoon pepper
2 (2½-ounce) jars sliced
   mushrooms, drained
1 (8-ounce) package thinly sliced
   country ham, cut into 1-inch
   pieces
4 slices bacon, cooked and
   crumbled (optional)
16 large eggs, lightly beaten
1 cup evaporated milk
¼ cup butter or margarine
   Garnish: chopped fresh parsley

Melt ¼ cup butter in a heavy saucepan over low heat; add flour, stirring until smooth. Cook, stirring constantly, 1 minute. Gradually add 1 quart milk; cook over medium heat, stirring constantly, until thickened and bubbly. Stir in pepper, mushrooms, country ham, and, if desired, bacon; remove from heat. Set aside.

Combine eggs and evaporated milk, stirring with a wire whisk.

Melt ¼ cup butter in a large nonstick skillet over medium heat; add egg mixture, and cook, without stirring, until egg mixture begins to set on bottom. Draw a spatula across bottom of skillet until eggs form large curds. Continue procedure until eggs are thickened but still moist; do not stir constantly. Remove from heat.

Spoon half of egg mixture into a lightly greased 13- x 9- x 2-inch baking dish; cover with half of ham mixture. Repeat procedure. (If desired, cover and chill 8 hours. Let stand at room temperature 30 minutes before baking.)

Bake, covered, at 300° for 30 minutes. Uncover and bake 30 additional minutes. Let stand 10 minutes. Garnish, if desired. **Yield:** 8 to 10 servings.

Peppered Pork Chop Casserole

6 (½- to ¾-inch-thick) bone-in
   pork chops
¼ teaspoon salt
¼ teaspoon pepper
2 tablespoons vegetable oil
2 medium-size green peppers
1 (15-ounce) can tomato sauce
1 (14½-ounce) can Italian-style
   stewed tomatoes, undrained and
   chopped
1 cup water
½ cup chopped onion
¾ teaspoon salt
¼ teaspoon pepper
1 clove garlic, minced
1½ cups long-grain rice, uncooked

Sprinkle pork chops with ¼ teaspoon salt and ¼ teaspoon pepper. Cook chops in hot oil in a large skillet over medium-high heat until browned on both sides; drain. Set aside.

Cut top off 1 green pepper; remove seeds. Cut 6 (¼-inch-thick) rings from green pepper; set rings aside. Seed and chop all remaining green pepper. Combine chopped pepper, tomato sauce, and next 6 ingredients; stir well.

Spread rice evenly in a lightly greased 13- x 9- x 2-inch baking dish. Pour tomato mixture over rice. Arrange pork chops over rice mixture; top each chop with a pepper ring.

Cover and bake at 350° for 1 hour or until chops and rice are tender. **Yield:** 6 servings.

Seafood Casserole

1 pound unpeeled, medium-size fresh shrimp
1 cup dry white wine
1 tablespoon butter or margarine
1 tablespoon chopped fresh parsley
1 teaspoon salt
1 medium onion, thinly sliced
1 pound fresh bay scallops
3 tablespoons butter or margarine
3 tablespoons all-purpose flour
1 cup half-and-half
½ cup (2 ounces) shredded Swiss cheese
2 teaspoons lemon juice
⅛ teaspoon pepper
½ pound crab-flavored seafood product
1 (4-ounce) can sliced mushrooms, drained
1 cup soft breadcrumbs
¼ cup grated Parmesan cheese
Paprika

Peel and devein shrimp; set aside.

Combine wine and next 4 ingredients in a Dutch oven; bring to a boil. Add shrimp and scallops, and cook 3 to 5 minutes; drain, reserving ⅔ cup liquid.

Melt 3 tablespoons butter in Dutch oven over low heat; add flour, stirring until smooth. Cook 1 minute, stirring constantly. Gradually add half-and-half; cook over medium heat, stirring constantly, until mixture is thickened and bubbly. Stir in Swiss cheese. Gradually stir in reserved ⅔ cup liquid, lemon juice, and pepper; add shrimp mixture, seafood product, and mushrooms.

Spoon mixture into a lightly greased 11- x 7- x 1½-inch baking dish. (If desired, cover and chill 8 hours. Let stand 30 minutes at room temperature before baking.)

Cover and bake at 350° for 40 minutes. Combine breadcrumbs and Parmesan cheese, and sprinkle over casserole; bake 5 additional minutes. Sprinkle with paprika; let stand 10 minutes before serving. **Yield**: 8 servings.

Gumbo Pot Pies

1 (2½-pound) broiler-fryer
2 quarts water
1 onion, quartered
2 bay leaves
½ cup all-purpose flour
½ cup vegetable oil
1 large green pepper, seeded and chopped
1 large onion, chopped
3 cloves garlic, chopped
2 pounds fresh or frozen okra, cut in ¾-inch slices
2 (10-ounce) cans whole tomatoes and green chiles
1 pound smoked andouille sausage, sliced
1 tablespoon dried thyme
1 pound unpeeled, large fresh shrimp
2 (17¼-ounce) packages frozen puff pastry, thawed
1 large egg, lightly beaten

Combine first 4 ingredients in a Dutch oven. Bring to a boil. Cover, reduce heat, and simmer 1 hour or until chicken is tender. Remove chicken, reserving 1½ cups broth; discard onion and bay leaves. Let chicken cool. Skin, bone, and coarsely chop chicken.

Combine flour and oil in a Dutch oven. Cook over medium heat, stirring constantly, 15 to 20 minutes or until roux is chocolate colored. Add green pepper, chopped onion, and garlic; cook, stirring constantly, 2 minutes. Add okra, tomatoes and green chiles, sausage, thyme, and reserved 1½ cups broth. Cover and simmer 30 minutes.

Peel and devein shrimp; stir shrimp and reserved chicken into gumbo, and cook just until shrimp turn pink. Remove gumbo from heat, and set aside to cool slightly.

Roll each pastry out on a lightly floured surface. Cut 4 circles out of each sheet of pastry, ½-inch larger than rims of individual 2-cup soup crocks. Return

pastry to freezer for at least 15 minutes. Cut decorative leaf or vine shapes with any excess pastry.

Ladle gumbo into individual crocks, filling three-fourths full. Brush top edges of pastry circles with beaten egg. Invert and place 1 pastry circle over each bowl, pressing firmly to sides of bowl to seal edges. Brush top of each with egg. Apply decorative leaves to top of pastry. Brush leaves with egg. Bake at 400° for 18 to 20 minutes or until pastry is puffed and golden. **Yield:** 8 servings.

Gumbo Pot Pie

Combine first 5 ingredients in a large skillet; cook over medium heat until sausage is browned and vegetables are tender, stirring until meat crumbles. Drain.

Stir in chicken broth and next 6 ingredients; spoon into a lightly greased 3-quart baking dish. Sprinkle with almonds.

Bake, uncovered, at 350° for 1½ hours. Let stand 5 minutes before serving. Garnish, if desired. Yield: 8 to 10 servings.

Wild Rice and Sausage

This hefty casserole actually tastes better with reduced-fat products. And it freezes nicely, so you can make it well ahead of time.

- 1 (16-ounce) package 60%-less-fat ground pork sausage
- 1 cup chopped celery
- 1 large onion, chopped
- 1 medium-size green pepper, seeded and chopped
- 1 clove garlic, minced
- 2 (14½-ounce) cans ready-to-serve chicken broth
- 1 (10¾-ounce) cans reduced-sodium, reduced-fat cream of mushroom soup, undiluted
- 1 (10¾-ounce) can reduced-sodium, reduced-fat cream of chicken soup, undiluted
- 1 (8-ounce) can sliced water chestnuts, drained
- 2 (4-ounce) cans sliced mushrooms, drained
- 1 (6-ounce) package long-grain-and-wild rice mix
- ¼ teaspoon dried thyme
- 1 (2-ounce) package sliced almonds
  Garnish: fresh parsley sprigs

Garden Lasagna

- ½ cup chopped celery
- 4 medium zucchini, coarsely chopped
- 3 cloves garlic, minced
- 1 large onion, chopped
- 1 medium-size green pepper, seeded and chopped
- 1 medium carrot, scraped and diced
- 3 tablespoons olive oil
- 2 (16-ounce) cans stewed tomatoes, undrained
- 1 (8-ounce) can tomato sauce
- 1 (6-ounce) can tomato paste
- ¼ cup chopped fresh parsley
- ¼ cup dry red wine
- 1 tablespoon dried Italian seasoning
- ½ teaspoon salt
- ¼ teaspoon freshly ground pepper
- 9 lasagna noodles, uncooked
- 1 (16-ounce) carton ricotta cheese
- 2 cups (8 ounces) shredded mozzarella cheese
- 1 cup grated Parmesan cheese

Cook first 6 ingredients in hot oil in a large Dutch oven over medium heat, stirring constantly, 15 minutes or until vegetables are tender. Stir in tomato and next 7 ingredients. Bring to a boil; cover, reduce heat, and simmer 30 minutes, stirring occasionally. Uncover and simmer 45 minutes or until sauce is thick, stirring occasionally.

Cook noodles according to package directions; drain. Spread one-fourth of sauce in a lightly greased 13- x 9- x 2-inch baking dish. Top with 3 noodles, one-third of ricotta cheese, one-fourth of mozzarella cheese, and one-fourth of Parmesan cheese; repeat layers twice. Top entire mixture with remaining one-fourth each of sauce, mozzarella cheese, and Parmesan cheese.

Bake, uncovered, at 350° for 35 to 40 minutes. Let stand 10 minutes before serving. **Yield**: 8 servings.

Mediterranean Ravioli

This one-dish meal is a vegetarian's dream. It's full of Italy's finest flavors.

   1 **(9-ounce) package refrigerated cheese-filled ravioli, uncooked**
   2 **cups peeled, cubed eggplant**
   1 **cup chopped onion**
   2 **cloves garlic, minced**
   2 **tablespoons olive oil**
   1 **(15-ounce) package refrigerated chunky tomato sauce**
   3 **tablespoons sliced ripe olives**
   1 **tablespoon balsamic vinegar**
   1 **teaspoon dried thyme**
  ⅔ **cup freshly grated Parmesan cheese**
      Garnishes: fresh basil sprigs, fresh thyme sprigs

Cook cheese-filled ravioli according to package directions; drain. Rinse with cold water; drain.

Cook cubed eggplant, chopped onion, and garlic in hot oil in a large skillet over medium-high heat, stirring constantly, until tender. Stir in tomato sauce and next 3 ingredients. Remove from heat.

Combine vegetable mixture and ravioli; toss gently. Spoon into a lightly greased shallow 2-quart baking dish. Cover and bake at 350° for 20 minutes. Uncover and sprinkle with cheese; bake, uncovered, 10 additional minutes or until thoroughly heated. Garnish, if desired. **Yield:** 4 servings.

Old-Fashioned Macaroni and Cheese

This is quintessential comfort food. It received the highest rating possible from our test kitchen critics.

   1 **(8-ounce) package elbow macaroni**
   3 **cups (12 ounces) shredded Cheddar cheese, divided**
   2 **large eggs, lightly beaten**
  1½ **cups milk**
  ¾ **teaspoon salt**
  ⅛ **teaspoon pepper**
      Paprika

Cook macaroni according to package directions; drain. Layer one-third of macaroni in a lightly greased 2-quart baking dish; sprinkle with 1 cup cheese. Repeat procedure with remaining two-thirds macaroni and 1 cup cheese, ending with macaroni. Reserve remaining 1 cup cheese.

Combine eggs and next 3 ingredients, stirring with a wire whisk or fork until blended. Pour mixture over macaroni. Cover and bake at 350° for 45 minutes or until thoroughly heated. Uncover and sprinkle with remaining 1 cup cheese and paprika. Cover; let stand 10 minutes before serving. **Yield:** 8 servings.

Chocolate Swirl Loaf, page 141

Great Tasting Gifts

Play Santa this year, and deliver a sleigh full of flavor-packed gifts. Flip through these pages for the perfect morsel. Then bake the gift, peek at the chapter's end for wrapping inspiration, and dream up some special packaging.

Mama Cle's Coffee Cake

A freshly baked cinnamon coffee cake has universal appeal.

½ cup butter or margarine, softened
½ cup shortening
1¼ cups sugar
2 large eggs
1 (8-ounce) carton sour cream
2 cups all-purpose flour
1 teaspoon baking powder
½ teaspoon baking soda
½ teaspoon salt
1 teaspoon vanilla extract
½ cup chopped pecans
2 tablespoons sugar
1 teaspoon ground cinnamon
Sifted powdered sugar

Beat butter and shortening at medium speed of an electric mixer 2 minutes or until creamy. Gradually add 1¼ cups sugar, beating at medium speed 5 to 7 minutes. Add eggs, one at a time, beating just until yellow disappears. Add sour cream, mixing until blended.

Combine flour and next 3 ingredients; gradually add to creamed mixture, mixing until blended. Stir in vanilla. Spoon half of batter into a greased and floured 8-inch tube pan.

Combine chopped pecans, 2 tablespoons sugar, and cinnamon; sprinkle half of pecan mixture over batter. Repeat procedure with remaining batter and pecan mixture.

Bake at 350° for 55 minutes. Let cool in pan on a wire rack 10 to 15 minutes; remove from pan, and let cool completely on wire rack. Sprinkle cake with sifted powdered sugar. **Yield:** one 8-inch coffee cake.

Apple Cake with Caramel Sauce

3 cooking apples, peeled, cored, and quartered
½ cup butter or margarine, softened
1 cup sugar
1 large egg
1 cup all-purpose flour
1 teaspoon baking soda
¼ teaspoon salt
1 teaspoon ground cinnamon
¾ teaspoon ground nutmeg
½ cup chopped pecans
Caramel Sauce

Position knife blade in food processor bowl, and add 4 apple quarters. Process 20 seconds or until finely chopped. Repeat procedure with remaining apple quarters to make 2½ cups chopped apple. Set mixture aside.

Beat butter at medium speed of an electric mixer in a large bowl until creamy. Gradually add sugar, beating well. Add egg; beat just until blended.

Combine flour and next 4 ingredients; add to butter mixture, stirring until blended. Stir in chopped apple and pecans. Spoon batter into a greased and floured wax paper-lined 9- x 5- x 3-inch loafpan.

Bake at 350° for 40 to 45 minutes or until a wooden pick inserted in center comes out clean. Let cool in pan on a wire rack 10 minutes. Remove from pan, and let cool completely on wire rack. Serve with Caramel Sauce. **Yield:** one 9-inch loaf.

Caramel Sauce
½ cup butter or margarine
1 cup firmly packed brown sugar
1 (5-ounce) can evaporated milk
1 teaspoon vanilla extract

Melt butter in a small saucepan over medium-low heat. Add brown sugar. Bring mixture to a boil, stirring constantly. Remove from heat. Stir in milk and vanilla. **Yield:** 1 cup.

Chocolate Swirl Loaves

6¾ to 7¼ cups all-purpose flour, divided
½ cup sugar
2 teaspoons salt
2 packages active dry yeast
1½ cups milk
½ cup butter or margarine
4 large eggs
¼ teaspoon ground cinnamon
2 (1-ounce) squares unsweetened chocolate, melted and cooled
Amaretto Glaze

Combine 2½ cups flour, sugar, salt, and yeast in a large mixing bowl; stir well. Combine milk and butter in a saucepan; heat until butter melts, stirring occasionally. Cool to 120° to 130°.

Gradually add liquid mixture to flour mixture, beating at low speed of an electric mixer until blended. Beat mixture 5 additional minutes at medium speed. Add eggs, beating well. Stir in enough remaining flour to make a soft dough.

Divide dough in half. Turn 1 portion of dough out onto a lightly floured surface; sprinkle with cinnamon, and knead until dough is smooth and elastic (about 8 to 10 minutes). Place in a well-greased bowl, turning to grease top. Cover and let rise in a warm place (85°), free from drafts, 1 hour or until doubled in bulk.

Turn remaining portion of dough out onto a lightly floured surface; pour melted chocolate over dough, and knead until dough is smooth and elastic and chocolate is incorporated (about 8 to 10 minutes). Place in a well-greased bowl, turning to grease top. Cover and let rise in a warm place, free from drafts, 1 hour or until doubled in bulk.

Punch each portion of dough down, and divide each portion in half. Roll 1 portion of chocolate dough and 1 portion of plain dough into 15- x 9-inch rectangles. Position chocolate rectangle on top of plain rectangle. Roll up, starting at short side, pressing firmly to eliminate air pockets; pinch ends to seal.

Place rolled dough, seam side down, in a well-greased 9- x 5- x 3-inch loafpan. Repeat procedure with remaining portions of chocolate and plain doughs.

Cover and let rise in a warm place, free from drafts, 1 hour or until doubled in bulk.

Bake at 350° for 45 minutes or until loaves sound hollow when tapped. Cover with aluminum foil the last 20 minutes of baking, if necessary, to prevent excessive browning. Remove from pans immediately; transfer to wire racks. Let cool 15 minutes. Drizzle Amaretto Glaze over warm loaves. **Yield:** 2 loaves.

Amaretto Glaze
2 cups sifted powdered sugar
2 tablespoons milk
1 tablespoon amaretto

Combine all ingredients in a small bowl, stirring until smooth. **Yield:** about 1 cup.

Lemon-Poppyseed Cake

Lemon-Poppyseed Cakes

Bake and deliver these gift loaves in reusable aluminum loafpans. You can find the pans at most grocery stores.

- 1 (18.25-ounce) package lemon cake mix without pudding
- 1 (3.4-ounce) package lemon instant pudding mix
- 1 cup water
- ½ cup vegetable oil
- 4 large eggs
- ½ cup chopped pecans
- 1 tablespoon poppyseeds
- 2 tablespoons sugar
- ½ cup lemon juice

Combine first 5 ingredients in a large mixing bowl; beat at medium speed of an electric mixer until blended. Stir in pecans and poppyseeds. Pour batter into 3 (8- x 3¾- x 2½-inch) greased reusable aluminum loafpans.

Bake at 325° for 40 minutes or until a wooden pick inserted in center comes out clean, shielding with aluminum foil after 30 minutes. Let cool in pans on wire racks 10 minutes.

Combine sugar and lemon juice; brush over cakes. Let cool completely on wire racks. Chill up to 1 week, or freeze up to 3 months. **Yield:** 3 loaves.

Butter-Pecan Turtle Bars

These gooey bars will receive widespread approval when you give them as gifts.

- ½ cup butter or margarine, softened
- 1 cup firmly packed brown sugar
- 2 cups all-purpose flour
- 1 cup chopped pecans
- ⅔ cup butter or margarine, melted
- ½ cup firmly packed brown sugar
- 1 cup (6 ounces) milk chocolate morsels

Beat ½ cup butter at medium speed of an electric mixer until creamy; add 1 cup sugar, beating well. Gradually add flour, mixing well. Press mixture into an ungreased 13- x 9- x 2-inch pan. Sprinkle with pecans; set crust aside.

Combine ⅔ cup butter and ½ cup brown sugar in a small saucepan. Bring to a boil over medium heat, stirring constantly. Boil mixture 30 seconds, stirring constantly. Remove from heat, and pour hot mixture over prepared crust.

Bake at 350° for 18 minutes or until bubbly. Remove from oven; immediately sprinkle with chocolate morsels. Let stand 3 minutes; cut through chocolate with a knife to create a marbled effect. Let cool. Cut into bars. **Yield:** 4 dozen.

Kahlúa Truffle Sticks

Here's an unforgettable cross between a truffle, a brownie, and fudge.

Softened butter
2 tablespoons sugar
1 (4-ounce) bar Swiss dark chocolate, chopped
3 (1-ounce) squares unsweetened chocolate, chopped
¼ cup plus 2 tablespoons butter or margarine, softened and divided
¾ cup sugar
2 large eggs
⅔ cup all-purpose flour
¼ teaspoon salt
⅓ cup Kahlúa
½ cup semisweet chocolate mini-morsels

Line a greased 8-inch square pan with aluminum foil, allowing foil to extend over edges. Grease foil with softened butter; sprinkle 2 tablespoons sugar onto foil. Set aside.

Combine chopped chocolate and 2 tablespoons butter in top of a double boiler; bring water to a boil. Reduce heat to low; cook until chocolate and butter melt. Remove from heat; let cool.

Beat remaining ¼ cup butter at medium speed of an electric mixer 2 minutes. Gradually add ¾ cup sugar, beating at medium speed 5 minutes. Add eggs, one at a time, beating until blended.

Combine flour and salt; add to butter mixture alternately with melted chocolate mixture and Kahlúa, beginning and ending with flour mixture. Mix at low speed just until blended after each addition. Stir in mini-morsels. Spoon batter into prepared pan.

Bake at 350° for 18 minutes. (Do not overbake.) Let cool completely. Cover and chill at least 2 hours.

Invert uncut brownies in foil onto a cutting board. Peel off foil. Invert brownies again. Using a sharp knife, cut into 2- x 1-inch sticks. **Yield**: 32 brownies.

Cinnamon-Pecan Icebox Cookies

1 cup butter or margarine, softened
¾ cup sugar
¼ cup firmly packed brown sugar
1 large egg
1 teaspoon vanilla extract
2¼ cups all-purpose flour
1½ teaspoons baking powder
½ teaspoon salt
1 cup finely chopped pecans
¼ cup sugar
1½ teaspoons ground cinnamon

Beat butter at medium speed of an electric mixer until creamy; gradually add ¾ cup sugar and ¼ cup brown sugar, beating well. Add egg and vanilla, beating well.

Combine flour, baking powder, and salt; add to creamed mixture, beating well. Stir in pecans. Cover and chill dough 2 hours. Shape into 2 (6- x 2½-inch) rolls. Wrap rolls in wax paper, and freeze until firm.

Combine ¼ cup sugar and cinnamon; stir well. Unwrap dough, and roll in sugar mixture. Slice frozen dough into ¼-inch-thick slices; place on ungreased cookie sheets. Bake at 350° for 12 minutes or until golden. Let cool on wire racks. **Yield:** 4 dozen.

Cookie Clue

• *The beauty of icebox cookies is that you can freeze the dough up to three months; then just slice and bake a few at a time.*

Cinnamon-Pecan Icebox Cookies

Wedding Cookies

These delicate gems with a hint of honey make a delightful dessert for a wedding reception or a baby shower.

¾ cup butter or margarine, softened
½ cup sifted powdered sugar
2 tablespoons honey
1 teaspoon vanilla extract
2 cups all-purpose flour
¼ teaspoon salt
½ cup finely chopped walnuts, toasted
Additional powdered sugar

Beat butter at medium speed of an electric mixer until light and fluffy; add ½ cup powdered sugar and honey, beating well. Stir in vanilla. Combine flour and salt; add to creamed mixture, mixing until well blended. Stir in walnuts.

Shape dough into 1-inch balls, and place 2 inches apart on lightly greased cookie sheets.

Bake at 325° for 12 minutes or until lightly browned. Let cool slightly on cookie sheets. Roll warm cookies in additional sugar. Let cool on wire racks. **Yield:** 3 dozen.

Apricot-Cheese Spread with Homemade Gingersnaps

¾ cup chopped dried apricots
¾ cup apricot nectar
⅓ cup raisins
⅓ cup chopped chutney
¼ cup brandy
½ teaspoon ground ginger
2 cups (8 ounces) shredded sharp Cheddar cheese
2 (8-ounce) packages cream cheese, softened
½ cup butter or margarine, softened
1⅓ cups finely chopped honey-roasted peanuts
Garnish: edible flowers
Homemade Gingersnaps

Combine first 6 ingredients in a small saucepan. Bring to a boil; reduce heat, and simmer, uncovered, 12 minutes or until thickened, stirring often. Transfer to a bowl; cover and chill.

Position knife blade in food processor bowl. Add cheeses and butter; process until smooth, scraping sides of processor bowl occasionally.

Line 2 (2½-cup) molds with heavy-duty plastic wrap. Spread ½ cup cheese mixture in bottom of each mold. Spread ¼ cup plus 2 tablespoons apricot mixture over cheese mixture in each mold. Repeat layers with ½ cup cheese mixture and half of remaining apricot mixture in each mold. Spread remaining cheese mixture evenly over each. Cover and chill thoroughly.

Unmold onto decorative plates; peel off plastic wrap. Press ⅔ cup peanuts gently onto each cheese mold. Garnish, if desired. Serve with Homemade Gingersnaps. **Yield:** 2 gift cheese molds.

Apricot-Cheese Spread
with Homemade Gingersnaps

Homemade Gingersnaps

Pair these crisp cookies with the nut-crusted cheese spread, and deliver them to a treasured friend.

³⁄₄ cup shortening
1 cup sugar
¹⁄₄ cup molasses
1 large egg
2 cups all-purpose flour
2 teaspoons baking soda
¹⁄₄ teaspoon salt
1 tablespoon ground ginger
¹⁄₂ teaspoon ground cinnamon
Additional sugar

Beat shortening at medium speed of an electric mixer until fluffy; gradually add 1 cup sugar, beating well. Add molasses and egg; mix well.

Combine flour and next 4 ingredients; mix well. Add about one-fourth of flour mixture at a time to creamed mixture, beating until mixture is smooth after each addition. Cover and chill at least 1 hour.

Shape dough into 1-inch balls; roll in additional sugar. Place 2 inches apart on ungreased cookie sheets.

Bake at 375° for 10 minutes. Let cool on wire racks. **Yield:** 4 dozen.

Homemade Coconut Granola

3½ cups regular oats, uncooked
½ cup grated coconut
½ cup sliced almonds
½ cup coarsely chopped pecans
½ cup wheat germ
¼ cup sesame seeds
¼ cup sunflower kernels
½ cup honey
¼ cup firmly packed brown sugar
¼ cup vegetable oil
½ cup crunchy peanut butter
1 teaspoon vanilla extract
¾ cup raisins (optional)

Combine first 7 ingredients in a large bowl. Stir well.

Combine honey, brown sugar, and oil in a small saucepan. Cook over medium heat, stirring until sugar melts and mixture is thoroughly heated. Remove from heat; add peanut butter and vanilla, stirring until blended. Drizzle over oat mixture; toss to coat. Spread mixture in a greased 15- x 10- x 1-inch jellyroll pan.

Bake at 250° for 50 to 60 minutes or until toasted and dry, stirring gently every 20 minutes; add raisins after 40 minutes, if desired. Let cool completely. Store mixture in an airtight container. **Yield:** 8 cups.

Variation: To make granola bars, press unbaked granola mixture (without raisins) into a greased 15- x 10- x 1-inch jellyroll pan, using greased fingertips. Press mixture flat with the back of a wide metal spatula. Bake at 250° for 1 hour and 20 minutes to 1½ hours or until toasted. Cut granola into bars while warm. Let cool completely in pan. Remove bars from pan, and store in an airtight container. **Yield:** 2½ dozen.

Parmesan Nuts and Bolts

3 cups corn-and-rice cereal
1 cup honey graham cereal or bear-shaped graham cereal
⅓ cup grated Parmesan cheese
¼ teaspoon garlic powder
1 (12-ounce) jar unsalted, dry-roasted peanuts
¼ cup butter or margarine, melted

Combine first 5 ingredients in a 15- x 10- x 1-inch jellyroll pan. Pour butter evenly over mixture; stir gently to coat.

Bake at 300° for 15 minutes, stirring every 5 minutes. Remove from oven; let cool. Store in an airtight container. **Yield:** 6¼ cups.

Honey and Spice Crunch

3 quarts popped corn
Vegetable cooking spray
3 tablespoons butter or margarine
¼ cup honey
¼ cup light corn syrup
3 tablespoons sugar
⅛ teaspoon salt
½ teaspoon ground cinnamon
¼ teaspoon baking soda
½ teaspoon vanilla extract
2 (0.9-ounce) packages dried fruit bits (about ½ cup)

Pour popcorn into a bowl coated with cooking spray; set aside.

Melt butter in a saucepan over low heat; stir in honey and next 3 ingredients. Bring to a boil over medium heat, stirring constantly. Boil, without stirring, 7 minutes or until a candy thermometer registers 250°.

Remove from heat; stir in cinnamon, soda, and vanilla; pour over popcorn, stirring to coat. Spoon mixture into a lightly greased 15- x 10- x 1-inch jelly-roll pan.

Bake at 250° for 25 minutes or until golden, stirring every 5 minutes. Stir in dried fruit. Let cool. Store in airtight containers. **Yield:** 3 quarts.

Herb-Cheese Croutons

Package these croutons and confit in a basket with a gift card that suggests serving them together. You might also include directions about storing them.

- 1 (13-ounce) package small soft breadsticks
- ¼ cup olive oil
- ¼ cup butter or margarine, melted
- 2 cloves garlic, minced
- ¼ cup grated Parmesan cheese
- 2 teaspoons dried Italian seasoning
- ¼ teaspoon ground red pepper

Slice bread with a serrated knife into ⅜-inch-thick rounds. Combine oil, butter, and garlic. Drizzle over bread rounds, tossing to coat. Combine Parmesan cheese, Italian seasoning, and pepper; sprinkle over bread rounds, tossing to coat.

Place on baking sheet; bake at 400° for 5 minutes. Turn rounds over, and bake 2 to 5 additional minutes or until crisp and brown. Let cool, and store in an airtight container up to 3 weeks. **Yield:** 10 cups.

Roasted Shallot-Garlic Confit

This aromatic dish takes its name, (kohn-FEE), from an old method of preserving. It's like a thick relish.

- ¼ cup butter, cut into pieces
- 2 tablespoons coarse sea salt
- 8 shallots, unpeeled
- 8 large cloves garlic, unpeeled
- 4 sprigs fresh thyme

Combine all ingredients in a small ovenproof skillet or pan; cover with aluminum foil.

Bake at 350° for 35 minutes or until shallots and garlic are tender. Remove shallots and garlic, reserving melted butter and discarding thyme and salt.

Peel and finely chop shallots and garlic. Stir melted butter into shallot mixture. Spoon into a small decorative jar. Store in refrigerator. Serve on crackers, French bread, toast, or croutons. **Yield:** about ½ cup.

Pepper Pecans

The light-colored Worcestershire sauce gives a more attractive coating to the pecans than does the darker sauce.

¼ cup golden Worcestershire sauce
2 tablespoons butter or margarine, melted
¼ teaspoon hot sauce
⅛ teaspoon pepper
2 cups pecan halves

Combine first 4 ingredients in a medium bowl; stir in pecans. Let stand 30 minutes.

Drain pecans, and spread in a single layer in a 13- x 9- x 2-inch pan.

Bake at 250° for 35 minutes, stirring every 10 minutes. Store in an airtight container up to 2 weeks. **Yield:** 2 cups.

Elf Gorp

8 cups popped corn
2 cups round crispy oat cereal
2 cups goldfish cracker pretzels
2 cups bite-size crispy rice cereal
1 cup peanuts
½ cup butter or margarine, melted
½ teaspoon seasoned salt
½ teaspoon garlic powder
1 tablespoon Worcestershire sauce

Combine first 5 ingredients in a large bowl. Combine butter, salt, garlic powder, and Worcestershire sauce in a small bowl; stir well. Pour over popcorn mixture; toss gently to coat, and pour into a large roasting pan.

Bake at 250° for 1 hour, stirring mixture at 15 minute intervals. Let cool completely; store gorp in an airtight container. **Yield:** 2½ quarts.

Peanut-Pretzel Mix

¾ cup butter or margarine, melted
2 to 3 tablespoons Worcestershire sauce
2 teaspoons garlic powder
1½ teaspoons curry powder
½ teaspoon ground red pepper
½ teaspoon chili powder
4 cups bite-size twisted pretzels
3 cups crispy corn cereal squares
2 cups shredded whole wheat cereal biscuits
1½ cups roasted peanuts

Combine first 6 ingredients in a small bowl; stir well. Combine pretzels and remaining 3 ingredients in a large bowl. Drizzle butter mixture over cereal mixture, stirring gently.

Spread mixture in 2 (15- x 10- x 1-inch) jellyroll pans. Bake at 350° for 10 to 12 minutes, stirring every 5 minutes. Remove from oven, and let cool completely. Store in an airtight container. **Yield:** 8 cups.

Chili Nuts

1 pound shelled raw peanuts
¼ cup peanut oil
1 tablespoon chili powder
1 teaspoon salt
¾ teaspoon paprika
½ teaspoon ground red pepper

Place peanuts in a shallow roasting pan; pour oil over nuts, stirring well. Roast peanuts at 350° for 35 minutes or until browned. Drain on paper towels. Combine chili powder and remaining 3 ingredients; sprinkle over peanuts, and stir until coated. **Yield:** about 2½ cups.

Smart Packaging

*Great-tasting recipes become even
more special when attractively packaged for giving.*

- *Package soft, chewy cookies* in breathable containers like cardboard bakery boxes. For a personal touch, collect Chinese take-out boxes, and decorate them with rubber stamps. (The stamps are available in variety stores in many designs.)

- Other creative containers for soft, chewy cookies include hat boxes, shoe boxes, Shaker boxes, or produce crates. Place wax paper between each layer of cookies. If packaging cookies in crates, first wrap them in plastic wrap.

- *Package crisp cookies*, hard candies, and crunchy savory nibbles in airtight containers like metal tins. Crisp foods will absorb moisture from the air if not stored in airtight containers.

- Embellish small metal coffee tins for packaging tiny truffles or other candies. Replace plastic tops to seal.

- Consider using an empty potato chip canister for packaging. Cover it with Christmas wrapping paper. Fill with crisp cookies, candies, or salty snacks, and replace its plastic top to seal.

- *Fill a Christmas stocking* with a favorite snack mix or nut mix. Just package the mix in large zip-top plastic bags. Tuck holiday napkins in the stocking.

- *Top off decorative jars of homemade dessert sauces* with raffia, or plaid or gold metallic ribbon and bows. Attach a homemade gift tag and an antique spoon. You can find collections of small spoons at flea markets and tag sales.

- *Package homemade breads* in lightweight recyclable aluminum pans available at most supermarkets. Wrap pans of bread with a large linen napkin. Or place bread in gift bags, and tie with ribbon.

- When giving a variety of foods together, *personalize a gift basket*. Include items to be eaten with your goodies or utensils that might be needed for further preparation. For example, package stone ground crackers and a block of cream cheese to serve with relish or chutney; or place bagels and a slicer alongside a gift of homemade preserves. Include a decorative butter knife, cookie cutters, hotpads, or a set of coasters. Round out your basket with flavored coffee or tea.

🍪 Baking Basics

*Our test kitchen staff has proven these hints
to be foolproof for any occasion.*

Measuring Up

*Measure ingredients accurately so your recipes will turn out the way you
want. Not all ingredients are measured with the
same type of equipment. Just follow these guidelines:*

• **Measure liquids** in glass or clear plastic measuring cups with rims above the last cup level to prevent spilling. Place the cup on a level surface (don't pick the cup up), and fill with liquid.

• **Measure dry ingredients** in metal or plastic measuring cups. Use the cup that holds the exact amount called for in the recipe.

• **Measure flour** by spooning it lightly into a dry measuring cup and letting it mound slightly; then level the top with a flat edge.

• **Cake flour** is the only flour that **needs sifting** before measuring; others are pre-sifted. Also, **sift powdered sugar** before measuring to remove lumps.

Cookie Scoop

- **If cookie dough is dry** and crumbly, stir in 1 to 2 tablespoons milk.

- **To prevent stiff cookie dough** from straining hand-held portable mixers, stir in the last few additions of flour mixture by hand.

- **If cookies spread too much** during baking, dough may be too soft. Put dough in refrigerator until well chilled. Also, let hot cookie sheets cool completely before reusing them.

- **If you don't have wire cooling racks** for cooling cookies, try this: Place wax paper on the counter, and sprinkle with sugar. Then place the cookies on sugared wax paper to cool.

- Sturdy bar cookies, drop cookies, and fruit cookies are the **best candidates for mailing**. Tender, fragile cookies are prone to crumbling when mailed. Use a heavy cardboard box as a mailing container, and pack and cushion it tightly so cookies don't shift around.

- **A tiny ice cream scoop** is a **handy gadget** that makes dropping dough onto cookie sheets a breeze (above). And you are guaranteed that all the cookies will be the same size.

The Take on Tarts

- The best way to be sure all **tartlet shells** are the **same size** is to divide dough in half; then pinch off equal-size mounds of dough to fill each muffin cup.

- Trace a small dessert plate or saucer to make a circle of dough for **an individual tart or pie**. And if you're in a pinch for a cookie cutter or biscuit cutter, use the rim of a drinking glass.

Cake Wisdom

- Use the correct pan size. Recipes suitable for a 10-inch tube pan, which holds 16 cups, won't always fit in a 12- or 13-cup Bundt pan.

- Beat butter and sugar 5 minutes with a heavy-duty stand mixer, 6 minutes with a standard mixer, or 7 minutes with a portable, hand-held mixer.

- Eggs should be room temperature when you add them to cake batter. To warm refrigerated eggs safely, run them, still in the shell, under warm water about 30 seconds.

- Preheat your oven 10 minutes before baking, unless otherwise specified.

- Stagger cakepans in the oven for even baking, and don't let pans touch.

- Bake cake layers on the center rack of oven unless recipe says otherwise.

Cake Pointers

Your cakes will turn out fluffy and fabulous if you follow the basic tips and suggestions on these pages.

Start with the Basics

- **Use shortening to grease cakepans,** when possible. Oil, butter, or margarine may cause cakes to stick or burn.

- **Dust greased cakepan with flour,** tilting to coat bottom and sides. Then shake out excess flour. This helps a baked cake come easily out of the pan.

Fine Finishes

- **Always frost the top of your cake last,** and keep frosting just ahead of the spatula as you spread so you don't drag crumbs from top of cake into frosting.

- **Here's an easy idea:** Place a doily over top of cake; then sprinkle cocoa, powdered sugar, or colored sugar over doily. Lift doily off to reveal a delicate design.

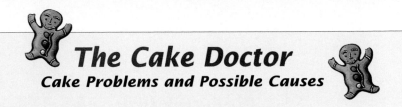

The Cake Doctor
Cake Problems and Possible Causes

If batter overflows:
- Overmixing
- Too much batter in pan

If cake falls:
- Oven not hot enough
- Undermixing
- Insufficient baking
- Opening oven door during baking
- Too much leavening, liquid, or sugar

If cake peaks in center:
- Oven too hot at start of baking
- Too much flour
- Not enough liquid

If crust is sticky:
- Insufficient baking
- Oven not hot enough
- Too much sugar

If cake sticks to pan:
- Cake cooling in pan too long
- Pan not greased and floured properly

If cake cracks and falls apart:
- Removing from pan too soon
- Too much shortening, leavening, or sugar

If texture is heavy:
- Overmixing when adding flour and liquid
- Oven temperature too low
- Too much shortening, sugar, or liquid

If texture is coarse:
- Inadequate mixing
- Oven temperature too low
- Too much leavening

If texture is dry:
- Overbaking
- Overbeating egg whites
- Too much flour or leavening
- Not enough shortening or sugar

High Altitude Adjustments

Cakes are affected by the lower air pressure at high altitudes more than any other type of baked good. When baked above 3,000 feet, cakes will not rise properly and may be dry and tough. Use this chart as a guide when baking cakes at high altitudes. In addition, when baking a cake above 3,000 feet in altitude, increase the baking temperature by 25°.

Ingredients	3,000 ft.	5,000 ft.	7,000 ft.	10,000 ft.
Sugar: *for each cup, decrease*	1 to 3 teaspoons	1 to 2 tablespoons	1½ to 3 tablespoons	2 to 3½ tablespoons
Liquid: *for each cup, add*	1 to 2 tablespoons	2 to 4 tablespoons	3 to 4 tablespoons	3 to 4 tablespoons
Baking Powder: *for each teaspoon, decrease*	⅛ teaspoon	⅛ to ¼ teaspoon	¼ teaspoon	¼ to ½ teaspoon

Piecrust Panache

Follow the tips and techniques below for your flakiest, most attractive pies ever.

Handling the Dough

- **Cut shortening** or cold butter pieces into flour mixture using a pastry blender. The mixture should form small clumps, which give your piecrust its flakiness.

- Here's one way to **get your pastry into the pieplate in one piece**: Roll pastry circle carefully onto a rolling pin; then lay the pin across top of pieplate, and unroll pastry into pieplate.

- Here's **another way to transfer pastry**: Fold pastry circle in half on a floured surface; then fold in half again. Lift pastry, place point in center of pieplate, and gently unfold.

Favorite Flutes

- **Cut a scalloped edge** for a piecrust by rolling the tip of a teaspoon around the edge of pastry after you transfer pastry to the pieplate.

- Give the scalloped edge a different look by gently **pressing a fork imprint** into each scallop. If fork sticks to pastry, dip it in flour.

- **Create a spiral fluted crust** by pressing the handle of a wooden spoon diagonally into the edge of chilled pastry at ½-inch intervals.

Recommended Storage

In Your Pantry
Packaged mixes

Cake mix	1 year
Casserole mix	18 months
Frosting mix	8 months
Pancake mix	6 months

Staples

Baking powder and baking soda	1 year
Flour	
All-purpose	10 to 15 months
Whole wheat, refrigerated	3 months
Milk	
Evaporated and sweetened condensed	1 year
Peanut butter	6 months
Salt, pepper, sugar	18 months
Shortening	8 months
Spices	
Ground	6 months
Whole	1 year
(Discard if aroma fades)	

In Your Refrigerator
Dairy

Butter and margarine	1 month
Buttermilk	1 to 2 weeks
Eggs	1 month
Half-and-half	7 to 10 days
Milk	
Whole and skimmed	1 week
Sour cream	3 to 4 weeks
Whipping cream	10 days

In Your Freezer
Quick Breads

Loaves, muffins, biscuits, coffee cakes, crêpes, pancakes, waffles	2 to 3 months

Yeast Breads

Loaves, rolls	3 to 6 months
Coffee cakes, sweet rolls	3 months
Doughnuts	1 month

Cakes

Unfrosted	2 to 5 months
Frosted with cooked frosting	not recommended
Frosted with creamy-type frosting	3 months
Cheesecakes	2 to 3 months

Cookies

Unfrosted cookies	8 to 12 months

Pastries

Cream puff shells	1 month
Puff pastry	6 months

Pies

Pastry shell	2 to 3 months
Fruit	1 to 2 months
Pumpkin	2 to 4 months
Custard, cream, meringue	not recommended

Dairy

Butter	6 months
Cheese	4 months
Ice cream	1 to 3 months
Eggs	
Whites	6 months
Yolks	8 months

Metric Equivalents

The recipes that appear in this cookbook use the standard United States method for measuring liquid and dry or solid ingredients (teaspoons, tablespoons, and cups). The information in the following charts is provided to help cooks outside the U.S. successfully use these recipes. All equivalents are approximate.

Metric Equivalents for Different Types of Ingredients

A standard cup measure of a dry or solid ingredient will vary in weight depending on the type of ingredient. A standard cup of liquid is the same volume for any type of liquid. Use the following chart when converting standard cup measures to grams (weight) or milliliters (volume).

Standard Cup	Fine Powder (ex. flour)	Grain (ex. rice)	Granular (ex. sugar)	Liquid Solids (ex. butter)	Liquid (ex. milk)
1	140 g	150 g	190 g	200 g	240 ml
¾	105 g	113 g	143 g	150 g	180 ml
⅔	93 g	100 g	125 g	133 g	160 ml
½	70 g	75 g	95 g	100 g	120 ml
⅓	47 g	50 g	63 g	67 g	80 ml
¼	35 g	38 g	48 g	50 g	60 ml
⅛	18 g	19 g	24 g	25 g	30 ml

Useful Equivalents for Liquid Ingredients by Volume

¼ tsp			=	1 ml	
½ tsp			=	2 ml	
1 tsp			=	5 ml	
3 tsp =	1 tbls		= ½ fl oz =	15 ml	
	2 tbls =	⅛ cup =	1 fl oz =	30 ml	
	4 tbls =	¼ cup =	2 fl oz =	60 ml	
	5⅓ tbls =	⅓ cup =	3 fl oz =	80 ml	
	8 tbls =	½ cup =	4 fl oz =	120 ml	
	10⅔ tbls =	⅔ cup =	5 fl oz =	160 ml	
	12 tbls =	¾ cup =	6 fl oz =	180 ml	
	16 tbls =	1 cup =	8 fl oz =	240 ml	
	1 pt =	2 cups =	16 fl oz =	480 ml	
	1 qt =	4 cups =	32 fl oz =	960 ml	
			33 fl oz =	1000 ml	= 1 l

Useful Equivalents for Dry Ingredients by Weight

(To convert ounces to grams, multiply the number of ounces by 30.)

1 oz	=	¹⁄₁₆ lb	=	30 g
4 oz	=	¼ lb	=	120 g
8 oz	=	½ lb	=	240 g
12 oz	=	¾ lb	=	360 g
16 oz	=	1 lb	=	480 g

Useful Equivalents for Length

(To convert inches to centimeters, multiply the number of inches by 2.5.)

1 in		=	2.5 cm	
6 in =	½ ft	=	15 cm	
12 in =	1 ft	=	30 cm	
36 in =	3 ft = 1 yd =		90 cm	
40 in		=	100 cm	= 1 m

Useful Equivalents for Cooking/Oven Temperatures

	Fahrenheit	Celcius	Gas Mark
Freeze Water	32° F	0° C	
Room Temperature	68° F	20° C	
Boil Water	212° F	100° C	
Bake	325° F	160° C	3
	350° F	180° C	4
	375° F	190° C	5
	400° F	200° C	6
	425° F	220° C	7
	450° F	230° C	8
Broil			Grill

Recipe Index

Recipe Index

Turn the page for more handy charts.

Favorite Baking Recipes

Cookies

_____
_____
_____
_____
_____

Cakes

_____
_____
_____
_____
_____

Pies

_____
_____
_____
_____
_____

Breads

_____
_____
_____
_____
_____

Snacks

_____
_____
_____
_____
_____